Miracles I Have Seen

Inscribed by

For Ron & Ruby Garrison

January, 2009

Number 79

Miracles I Have Seen

Enlarged Second Edition of
The Way Things Used to Be

By Louis Arnold

Arnold Publications
2440 Bethel Road
Nicholasville, KY 40356

Miracles I Have Seen
© 2008 Louis Arnold
Published by Arnold Publications
Enlarged Second Printing
All rights reserved, except for brief quotations
embodied in critical articles and reviews.
Library of Congress Card Number: 2008909620

ISBN: 978-0-9727188-7-5
Printed in the United States of America

Arnold Publications
2440 Bethel Road
Nicholasville, Kentucky 40356
Phone (859)858-3538
Toll free (800)854-8571

Dedicated to the memory of Edward Lawrence Arnold
and Texie Agee Arnold, my father and mother,
whose exemplary examples instilled
in me the value of hard work,
right living, and integrity.

Contents

The Good Old Days
L. Walker Arnold

I long for the good old days,
   When a man's word was his bond,
And a handshake sealed a deal
   As good as the touch of a magic wand.

I long for the days when a dirty word
   Made one blush and look askance,
And Mama threatened to wash with soap
   That dirty mouth when she got a chance.

Back then, girls were sweet and innocent,
   And as pure as the driven snow,
So we placed them on a pedestal,
   And hoped our crudeness wouldn't show.

Now the good old days have passed me by.
   It's almost like they've never been,
But I can never forget those days
   When ladies were ladies and men were men.

Introduction to
Miracles I Have Seen

M*iracles I Have Seen* is a rewrite of my book, *The Way Things Used to Be*. It contains memories of events in my life, just as the first edition did, but there is an added emphasis on some miracles I have seen God perform.

Chapters 2 and 3 cover some miracles in my early life. Chapters 4 through 13 contain memories of my experiences growing up. Chapter 14 and following tell about miracles I have experienced in my years in the ministry.

We see few miracles today because we attempt few things that require miracles. God does not perform miracles when no miracles are needed. Natural means can solve most of the problems and meet most of the needs we have today, so there is no need for miracles. If God answered our prayers for miracles that are not needed, they would become so commonplace they would no longer be considered miracles.

In the past God only performed miracles when miracles were needed. He did not shut the mouths of the lions until Daniel was in their den. He did not cool the fire in the furnace until the three Hebrew children were cast into it. He did not rain manna from Heaven for the Israelites to eat while they were in Egypt, and He stopped raining manna from Heaven when they reached Canaan and were able to eat the corn of the land.

And the manna ceased on the morrow, after they had eaten of the old corn of the land; neither had the children of Israel manna any more; but they did eat of the fruit of the land of Canaan that year (Josh. 5:12).

Not all miracles are outstanding. Some are small, but they are needed nonetheless. In Bible times God performed both small miracles and great miracles. It was a small miracle when God sent ravens to feed Elijah in the wilderness. It was a great miracle when He sent a chariot of fire to carry him home to Heaven. It was a small miracle when God answered Gideon's prayer and made his fleece wet with dew while the ground around it remained dry, and, on the next night, made the ground wet and the fleece dry. It was a big miracle when God used Gideon and three hundred men with trumpets, lamps and pitchers to put a Midianite army to flight.

It was a small miracle when Elisha caused the axe head that had been lost in the river to swim. It was a large miracle when Naaman dipped in the Jordan seven times and was cleansed of his leprosy.

It was a great miracle when God parted the Red Sea so the Israelites would escape from Pharaoh's army. It was a small miracle when Moses healed the bitter water of Marah so the people could drink. When Elisha increased the oil for a widow of a son of the prophets, it was a small miracle, but it was a greatly needed miracle. She sold the oil and paid her debts so her sons were not sold into slavery.

It was a small miracle when Jesus sent Peter to catch a fish with enough money to pay his taxes, but it was a needed miracle.

In this day we are attuned to the world of material things, but we must not forget that God is a God of power and that He still performs miracles when they are needed.

We must not forget that every time a person is born again that is a miracle of redeeming grace. We have all seen that manifested in changed lives. When a person lives a consistent, godly life that is another miracle. When God uses someone in a special way, that too is a miracle.

I claim no credit for any of the events that I recount in this book. Recognizing my weakness, I say with Paul, "*. . . who is sufficient for these things?" (2 Cor. 2:16).* Then I add, as Paul did, *". . . our sufficiency is of God" (2 Cor. 3:5).*

As I write these lines I am 94 years old. I have not retired or slowed down very much. It is a continuing miracle that God keeps me busy traveling, preaching, and writing.

I do not hesitate to tell of miracles I have seen because God wants people to know that He is a miracle-working God. He instructed the people of Israel to "*. . . make known his deeds among the people" (1 Chr. 16:8).*

Our God wants us to know that He is a miracle-working God, and He wants us to attempt great things for Him. When we do He can do great things for us.

Chapter 1

Clearing Away the Brush

It seems only yesterday that I was a bare-foot boy chasing a hoop down a dusty lane. Now they call me a senior citizen. Someone has said there are four stages in a man's life. There is the stage when he is a baby and ladies look at him and say, "My, isn't he cute." A few years later teenage girls look at him and sigh, "He's cool." Then there comes the stage when his peers look at him and say, "You're looking good." What they really mean is, "You look better than I thought you would at your age." Then there is the time when people look at a man and say, "Doesn't he look natural."

I can hardly believe that I have reached the stage in life when my peers tell me I'm looking good, and children look up at me and say, "Gee, he's old." I don't feel old, but I'll have to admit that a lot of water has gone under the bridge since that country boy chased a hoop down a lane. I started life in horse-and-buggy days. Now we travel in jet aircraft and send men into space. My father used to hoot at the suggestion that men would one day go to the moon in a rocket, but I have lived to see men walk on the moon!

When I was a boy we used to stand on the hill in front of our house and call to our neighbor on the next hill at the top of our voices. Now we communicate by radio, cellular phones, fax machines, e-mail, and voice mail. We even see what is happening on the other side of the earth by way of satellite and television.

I started life in a house that was dimly lit by kerosene lamps. Now our houses and our cities blaze with electric lights. We used to write, figure, and keep records by dipping scratchy pens in bottles of ink and dragging them across pages that had to be blotted from time to time and usually looked messy when we finished. Now we do our writing, figuring, and record keeping with computers.

In my lifetime we have progressed in heating our homes, from the fireplace to Warm Morning Heaters, to furnaces, to solar heat, and to heat pumps. In entertainment, we have gone from the victrola, with the big morning-glory horn, to radio, television, and CD players. Motion pictures used to be flickering black and white images, projected on a silver screen. The film was highly flammable and often caught fire during projection. The pictures were silent, so one had to read the messages projected on the screen to know what the characters were saying. Now we have televisions that brings news and entertainment into our homes in color, high definition, and stereo sound.

My generation has seen more change than any generation of the past. Sadly, those of us who have lived to see so many changes are now a dying generation, and the memory of how people lived before those changes came will die with us if we do not leave some written records. So, with some trepidation, I have decided to chronicle a few memories of those changes. I trust that will help my own generation to remember how things were when they were growing up and that it will give those who come after us an idea of the days through which we have lived.

This book is largely autobiographical, for I cannot write about my memories without writing about my life. Many have asked me to write my life's story, but until the writing of the first edition of this book I deferred to do so. In the first edition I related some selected memories from my long and extremely busy life. In this edition I have added some miracles I have seen God perform. As stated in the introduction, I have changed the title of the book from *The Way*

Things Used to Be to *Miracles I have Seen.* Some of the material in this book has been previously published in *The Arnold Report*, under the caption, *I Remember.* The memories I have shared in *The Arnold Report* were so well received, I decided that they should be enlarged upon and preserved in more permanent form. I hope that in this form these memories will be enjoyed by more people in my generation and by others in generations to come.

This book could be called my memoirs. It is that—somewhat. It could be called the history of my time, for it does contain a bit of the history of the years through which I have lived. The book is somewhat a record of the discoveries and inventions of the twentieth century, for they have been the greatest years of discovery and invention in the history of the world. This book could be called a book of nostalgia, for it harks back to a quieter, simpler time.

I trust that my readers will enjoy wandering down the trails of memory with me. I trust also that some of the younger generation will enjoy reading the way people lived in past generations, and I pray that the miracles I have written about will cause them to believe in the God of miracles. I have seen my share of miracles, but I take no credit for them. Only God can perform miracles.

Chapter 2

The Miracle of My Birth

I was born January 17, in the little village of Buckeye, Kentucky. According to my mother I was born on a cold, winter day. That was more years ago than I care to remember, but I find many people who are wondering how old I am. I wonder why. I'm the one who should be concerned about my age.

To those who are curious, I will only say what I said to a nosy school teacher when I was in the first grade. Or was it the second grade? The teacher asked me when I was born, and I promptly replied, "I do not remember." Then I wondered why everyone in the classroom laughed.

For those who are not satisfied with that answer, I will say that I can remember the Vietnam War, the Korean Conflict, WWII and some talk of WWI, but, try as I will, I cannot remember the Civil War. Seriously, I was born in 1914. You can calculate my present age from that.

I was born the son of Edward Lawrence Arnold (Ed) and Texie Agee Arnold. My father was a village blacksmith at the time of my birth, but he later became a farmer and remained one until he retired at the age of seventy-two.

My mother was a simple Christian housewife who had never heard of "Women's Lib." She would not have been interested if she had, for she was already as liberated as she wanted to be. She was free to love her husband, her child, and her home. She was free to read her Bible, to pray, and to attend church. She was free to be a homemaker, and she never dreamed of being a homebreaker. She was free to love her neighbors and to share what she had with them. She was free to bring her son to know the Lord, free to train him, free to pray for him, and free to instill in him the desire to serve God and to amount to something in the world.

Now, lest I get ahead of myself, it is best that I go back to the beginning of the story.

My mother was one of three daughters born to Farris and Emily Masters Agee. Her sisters were Lena and Ina. She was born in Madison County, Kentucky, but her family moved to Garrard County, where she grew up. She attended a country church with her family, and became a Christian at an early age.

My Mother's Dedication

From the time my mother was saved, She wanted to do something definite for the Lord. There were things she knew she could not do, for her education was limited, and she was not strong in body. She finally decided that the Lord wanted her to be a wife and the mother of a baby boy that would become a preacher. She surrendered her life for that purpose, and, like Hannah of old, she promised that if ever she had a son, she would dedicate him to the Lord. That decision became the guiding principle of her life.

Courting in the Old Days

In time Ed came courting at the Agee home, as young men did in those days. He did not drive up in an automobile, honk the horn out front and wait for Texie to come out. Instead, he rode up on horseback, dismounted, hitched his horse at the fence, crossed the stile, went to the front door of the house, and knocked.

As was the custom in those days, Texie's mother probably opened the door and invited Ed to come in and have a seat in the parlor. "Texie will be ready in a few minutes," she probably said.

Ed probably thanked her, entered the parlor

and sat down.

Texie had most likely been ready and waiting for some time, but in those days it was thought proper to keep a young man waiting a decent length of time.

In due time Texie entered the parlor and the young couple greeted. As was the custom, Texie's mother retired to a room not too far away, while the young couple courted.

Somebody has said that back then, the old mantle clock with the swinging pendulum seemed to say, "Take your time. Take your time." At a later day, the alarm clock, ticking on the dresser, seemed to say, "Get together quick. Get together quick." Now we have silent clocks, except when they alarm, and then they only make a strange beeping sound, so they really don't say anything. The television is not silent though, and it often blasts away with the home-destroying message that young couples need not even bother with getting married.

It was a different world when Ed and Texie courted in the parlor or rode their horses to church on Sundays. When they rode to church, Texie rode a sidesaddle and wore a riding habit that was long enough to cover her ankles, lest young men see too much. Now it seems the fear is that they will see too little.

Despite the restrictions of those days, the courting got done, and in due time the man who was to be my father proposed to the girl who was to be my mother. I know not whether it was in the parlor or in some shaded nook where they stopped their horses on the way to church. I only know that one day he said, "Wilt thou?" and she said, "I wilt."

My Parents' First Home

In due time my dad and mother married and moved into a small house across the road from Liberty Baptist Church at Buckeye, Kentucky where Ed had his blacksmith shop.

Blacksmithing was not an easy way to make a living, but my father was not afraid of hard work. Yet, despite his hard work, the blacksmith shop did not prosper. He was easy going, and he could not turn down those who wanted their horses shod or their farm tools mended on credit. Times were hard, and payments for services done on credit were slow. He could seldom bring himself to the point of asking that an account be paid, so all too often they remained unpaid.

That was not the only worry Texie had. Ed was not a Christian, and she must have had many heartaches as she prayed for a husband who was living in sin and seldom went to church. Ed did not pray, but he swore easily and often.

However, Texie had one thing to cheer her during the first year of her marriage. She believed that she would soon fulfill her promise to the Lord by bearing a son who would become a preacher.

At last the day arrived, and my mother gave birth to a baby boy, but, to her sorrow, he did not live. Her sorrow was made even greater when the doctor told her she could never bear another child and live. Her only recourse was to go to the Lord in prayer.

In time the conviction grew that, no matter what the doctor said, the Lord wanted her to be the mother of a preacher. So she prayed that the Lord would give her another baby boy, and that he would live.

The Miracle of My Birth

In time I was born, and I lived. That was the first of many miracles relating to my life. Later, my mother gave birth to another baby boy, but he did not live. I was the only one of her three babies that lived. The baby born before me was born dead, and the baby boy born after me was born dead. So it was a miracle that I lived.

After I was born, my mother was confined to her bed for many days. Years afterward she told me that she had crawled to my crib on her hands and knees as soon as she was able and had buried her face in my body, and, with tears streaming down her cheeks, dedicated me to God.

My Mother's Influence

When I was growing up, my mother prayed for me and taught me the Word of God. I do not remember when I did not know that the Bible is the Word of God. Nor can I remember when I did not know that I needed to be saved. My bedtime stories were from the Bible, and my lullabies were the old hymns. To this day, in my mind, I can hear my mother singing as she went about the house, *I Come to the Garden Alone.* I love that song to this day.

My mother prayed for me until God saved me. Then she prayed until I answered the call to preach. After I was in the ministry, she continued to pray for me. She prayed for me as long as she lived, and I believe that in Heaven she is still praying for me.

Chapter 3

The Devil Wanted Me Dead

My birth was a miracle, but that was only the beginning of my battle for life. While I was yet an infant, an epidemic of smallpox swept our community, and I came down with that dread killer disease. I was not expected to live, but I did, and that was a miracle.

Also in my infancy, I had a disease called scrofula, a swelling in the neck caused by tuberculosis of the lymph nodes in that area. I was sick for a long time and suffered a great deal, I was told when I was old enough to understand.

Finally the doctor decided to lance my neck. He must have come close to cutting my head off, for a scar on my neck remains to this day. I may have come close to dying, but I lived. That was another miracle.

In my boyhood I was skinny and delicate, and I was frequently ill with the usual childhood diseases. I also had several bouts with appendicitis in my preteen years. It is strange that they never rushed me to surgery. I spent many days in bed with my knees drawn up against my stomach to ease the pain, and I had frequent times of nausea. It is also strange that my appendix did not rupture. If it had, I would most likely have died. I never had an operation for my diseased appendix, but somehow I lived through the pain and suffering, and eventually I got over it. Satan wanted me dead, ". . . *but God meant it unto good . . .*"

Between my bouts of sickness, I was very active. I ran and jumped and played like other boys, and I spent long hours exercising and trying to build up my health. Somewhere I had heard that President Teddy Roosevelt had been delicate in health as a boy and that through exercise he had built a robust body and abundant health. So I exercised whenever I was able.

By the time I reached my teen years my health was better, so Satan tried different tactics. He tried to get me killed.

Shot at by a Neighbor

One night I went hunting with my dogs, carrying a lantern as I always did. It was the custom back then to hunt on neighboring farms without prior notice, so with no thought of danger, I climbed a fence and started across a neighbor's farm. I had hunted on this farm before, both alone and in company with others. Never had this farmer, or any other farmer in the community, offered the least objection to our hunting on their land. But on this night, I saw a light go on in the farmhouse, and a moment later someone raised a window and fired two shots at me in quick succession. Bullets thudded into the ground at my feet. It didn't take me long to get over the fence and away from that neighbor's farm. Satan wanted me dead, "... *but God* ..."

Shot at Again

Before television, or even radio had been invented, young people often met in a home to have a party. A party back then did not mean drinking liquor or shooting dope, though some roughnecks did sometimes go outside and take a nip of "moonshine" from a fruit jar. A party in those days was for playing games, telling stories, asking and answering riddles, making pull candy, laughing, and playing music and singing.

One night, as a friend and I were walking home from a party, a young man waylaid us and shot at us twice. I heard the bullets whiz past me, and thud into a high bank by the side the road. They must have only missed me by inches. Satan wanted me dead, "... *but God* ..."

I thought I knew who had done the shooting, so the next day I went to see him. "Here are the two shells you wasted shooting at me last night," I said, offering them to him. He didn't take the shells, but he didn't deny shooting at me either.

Saved by a Rib

Soon after this a young man came to our farm and started a fight with me. My mother had taught me to never start a fight, but never to run if one could not be avoided. The young man decided that he should do the running, and I called after him to never come back on our property again. This may not have been the right thing to do. I am just telling the way it happened.

Soon he came back looking for trouble. I did not know he was hiding an open knife behind his back when he started the fight. I did not back off, and he struck for my heart with the knife. The blade went through my jacket directly over my heart. I was turning as it struck, so the knife went through my under jacket a bit lower. The hole it cut in my shirt was still lower. The blade went through my underwear directly above my lower rib. It cut through the flesh and hit the rib bone. That stopped it from penetrating the cavity of my body. If his knife had hit where he aimed it, I would have died on the spot. Adam's rib gave him a wife. My rib saved my life. Satan wanted me dead," *. . . but God . . .*"

A Year of Sickness

After I had grown-up and gone into the ministry, I had more illnesses. In one year I had typhoid fever, whooping cough, and kidney stones. (Imagine a grown man having whooping cough.) About that time I also had mumps, but all that was not the worse of my sickness. I also had to have my tonsils taken out. The doctor took them out with me sitting on a stool in his office. He put a shot in my throat to numb the pain, but it had no effect. I thought he was cutting my head off while he was taking my tonsils out. Somehow I lived through the pain and recovered without the doctor seeing me again.

A Fatal Illness

Shortly after that, a doctor discovered that I had Bright's disease. I'm sure they have another name for the disease now.It was an incurable disease at that time, and the doctor frankly told me that I did not have long to live. I did not believe him, so I went to another doctor. He gave me the same diagnosis and told me that I would not live long. Still unbelieving, I went from doctor to doctor. (It was fortunate for me that doctors did not charge preachers in those days). I visited at least seven doctors, and only one of them gave me any hope. He treated me for some time, then one day he told me he had done all he could for me. "You only have a short time to live," he told me. "I suggest that you quit the ministry. Go out west and take it easy. Enjoy the little time you have left. It won't be long."

I walked out of his office feeling that I had received a death sentence. I did not question what he told me. By that time the disease had so ravished my body, it was evident that I was dying. I only weighed 123 pounds, and I was so weak I could barely walk from my parsonage across a small lawn to the front door of my church and down the aisle to the pulpit. By the time I had preached 15 minutes, I was completely exhausted, and it was all I could do to get back to the parsonage and get in the bed. I had to rest all afternoon to be able to preach that night. I was almost too weak to drive my automobile, and when I did my vision often blacked out. It is a wonder I was not killed in an accident. Satan wanted me dead," *. . . but God . . .*"

A Different Doctor

I will never know where I got the faith to pray for my healing. I only know that one dark night, about two o'clock in the morning, I called in another Doctor.

I had not slept. I was so weak I could barely get out of bed and on my knees. I remember praying something like this: "Dear Lord, You have called me to preach, and I do not believe my ministry is over. My doctor has told me to quit the ministry, but I don't believe You want me to quit. Lord, I can't go on preaching the way I am, so I pray that You will heal me. I don't care whether You give me new kidneys or repair the ones I have. I just want You to heal me."

I didn't hear any bells or whistles, but a sense of peace came to my heart, and a feeling of well-being came to my body. I got back into bed, fell asleep, and slept like a baby until the next morning. When I awoke, I felt better than I had in months. I decided to forget the restricted diet I was on and eat like a normal person. Eating must have agreed with me, for I started gaining weight. According to a record I kept of answered prayers back then, I gained 32 pounds in the next month. I recall that by that time I was feeling well. Nonetheless, I decided to go to a specialist for a checkup. The specialist ran his tests, then told me to go for a walk and to come back in about an hour. When I returned, he gave me good news.

"I don't know what you have had, but there is nothing wrong with you now," he told me.

I left his office thanking and praising God for

health to go on with my ministry. It has been many years since then, and my disease has not returned. My healing was truly a miracle. Satan wanted me dead, "*. . . but God . . .*"

Chapter 4

Boyhood Days

I grew up on a rock-strewn, gully-washed, hill farm with a weathered barn and a crude little house, but I still found much beauty to enjoy. There were summer mornings when the sun came up like a golden lamp and made the dewdrops sparkle like diamonds in the meadow and on the morning glory and the trumpet flowers that grew in the fence rows. At noon the sunbeams danced on the riffles in the creek, and in the late afternoon they painted the western sky in shades of pink and red and gold, and when rain clouds appeared the sun painted a rainbow on them.

The creek at the foot of the hill was filled with minnows and tadpoles, and the pool below the house was the home of green and brown bullfrogs. Snake doctors (dragonflies) darted in the air around the pool and along the creek, and butterflies danced in the air above Mama's flower garden in the side yard.

In the winter the farm was often covered with a blanket of frost-covered snow that sparkled in the sunlight, and I often looked out my window in the early morning through icicles that hung like great snaggled teeth from the eaves of our house.

The blooming of buttercups in the early spring brought the promise of warmer weather, and a bit later the peach, plum, and apple trees hung out their blossoms, telling us that spring had arrived.

In the fall the hickory nut and walnut trees were loaded with nuts, and the maple, oak, and beech trees, turned to colors of red and gold and yellow and brown and rust.They shook their heads in the autumn wind, and their leaves drifted down like tiny sails.

I seldom crossed the borders of our county when I was growing up. The only times I did were when my grandmother took me in her buggy to Richmond in Madison County.

In manhood, I have seen mighty oceans rocking in their beds: restless, beautiful, and terrible. I have seen great rivers flowing through verdant valleys, with mighty mountains towering above them and stabbing at the clouds. I have seen smoking volcanoes under cloud-fleeced skies, wildflowers blossoming in tropical jungles, and birds, plumed with feathers of every hue, darting and wheeling through jungles of trees and tangled vines. But nothing I have seen holds more for me in memory than the old home place where I grew up.

In my growing up years we knew nothing of toast and coffee for breakfast, salad for lunch, and dinner in the evening. At breakfast we ate ham, red-eyed gravy, eggs, and hot biscuits with blackberry jam, apple jelly, or sorghum molasses. At noon, in the summertime, we ate fried chicken from our own flock. In the fall, during the hunting season, we killed rabbits and ate them for dinner or supper. In the spring, before our chickens came on, we hunted and shot young rabbits, even though it was out of season.

In the winter we ate steak or pork from animals we had raised on the farm. In the early spring we went wild-greens picking on our farm and on neighboring farms. A bit later we had onions, lettuce and radishes from our early garden, and from rows we had planted along the edge of the tobacco beds. When the summer garden came on, we had "taters" and beans, "maters" and corn and squash. Also, we had butter beans, green beans and melons in season. We always had biscuits or cornbread with our meals. We had coffee and milk the year around, and in the summer we had iced tea, if the ice we had brought from town on Saturday had not all melted.

Supper was a special time. We had finished the hard work for the day, fed the animals, milked the cow, gathered the eggs from the nests, and carried water from the spring. Now we could relax and enjoy the good meal Mama had prepared.

We ate by lamplight because electricity had not yet reached our community. When Mama finished cooking supper she moved the kerosene lamp from the shelf to the center of the table. Then she set our plates on the table and put the food on, and we drew up our chairs and sat down to eat.

The Family Bible

When we finished eating Mama removed the dishes and food and brought the family Bible to the table. Sometimes Papa would read aloud from the Bible, though he did not read very well. Usually Mama read to Papa and me. I liked it better when Mama read. After the Bible reading was finished, we usually remained at the table for a time, talking about what had been read. Often one of us would raise a question, and we would try to come up with an answer. I learned much from the Bible in this way, and by the time I was grown, I had a general knowledge of what was in the Bible.

When bedtime came Mama picked up the

lamp and led the way to my bedroom. She placed the lamp on the mantle, then knelt beside me while I said my bedtime prayer. After I had prayed, she would go out, promising to come back and tuck me in after I got in bed. I will never forget her good night kiss and the way she pulled the cover up around my shoulders. After she left with the lamp, it seemed that angels came down and hovered around my bed. I doubt that my mother realized that she was building memories that would last me for a lifetime.

I Loved Fishing

One of the happiest memories of my childhood was fishing in the nearby ponds and creeks. Papa first took me fishing when I was a small boy. He had been promising to take me for some time, and finally he set an afternoon when we would go. I am sure that, as we worked in the field that morning, I must have reminded him of his promise several times.

After dinner I went out with Papa to make preparations to go fishing. Our preparations were simple and primitive, but I could not have been more excited. Money was scarce in those days, so instead of buying fishing tackle, we made our own.

We went to the cane thicket, a quarter mile

from the house, and cut the tallest canes we could find for fishing poles. Then we made fishing lines from some of Mama's #9 sewing thread. We made the line by twisting the thread and doubling it a couple of times to make it strong enough to land the fish we hoped to catch. We made hooks of bent pins. We found small stones and tied them to the lines for sinkers, and we used short sections of pith from last year's cornstalk for bobbers. We called them floaters. After we finished making our fishing tackles and wound the lines around our cane poles, we got an empty tin can and a grubbing hoe and went to dig worms for bait.

We were only going to fish for one afternoon, but Papa dug enough worms for a week of fishing. I was so eager to start fishing, I thought we would never reach the creek, but we finally did. Then, carrying the can of worms and our fishing poles, Papa led the way. We soon came to a fence near the creek. We climbed over the fence and went to a likely spot on the creek bank. There Papa unwound my line, baited my hook and threw the line out in the water as far as he could with the cane pole.

"Now watch the floater," he told me. "If it starts bobbing up and down jerk the pole and you'll catch a fish."

He had scarcely finished his instructions when my bobber started bouncing in the water. My heart almost stopped, and I jerked the pole as hard as I could. If the tackle had been sufficient, and if I had been strong enough, I could have landed a whale. As it was, I threw a tiny catfish over the fence and into the field behind me.

I scrambled over the fence and retrieved my tiny fish, and Papa cut a willow switch, strung my fish on it, and fastened it to the creek bank. The fish disappeared beneath the water at once, but I soon pulled it up for another look. I was sure there had never been a more beautiful fish than the one I had caught.

In manhood I have fished in rivers, lakes and oceans. I have fished from shores, bridges, boat docks and boats. I have caught game fish, some of them large, but I have never had a bigger thrill than I did the day I caught my first fish.

Papa and I fished often after that, and we caught far larger fish than my first one. I also fished alone and in the company of others my age. We fished in ponds, creeks and in a rock quarry. Often I caught a stringer full of tiny sunfish, and late in the afternoon I proudly carried them home. I cleaned them and Mama fried them for supper. She always fried them crisp and brown so we could eat them bones and all.

I still enjoy fishing, though I now seldom have time or opportunity to fish. For many years the business of my life has been fishing for men. I have had some great thrills in catching fish, but they do not compare with the thrill of catching men. I am thankful that my dad taught me to fish for fish. I am even more thankful that my Saviour has taught me how to catch men. Jesus said to his disciples, *". . . from henceforth thou shalt catch men" (Luke 5:10).* Again He said to them, *". . . Follow me, and I will make you fishers of men" (Matthew 4:19).* Fishing for men has been my calling and my life's work, and I believe that all I experienced in my childhood and young manhood helped to prepare me for my life's work.

Chapter 5

I Knew Hard Times

When I was growing up they said that times were hard, but we didn't start a riot, or ask the government to support us. The government didn't have a poverty program in those days, but we had our own. We worked!

We raised a garden and ate from it in the summer. We canned enough from it to last through the winter. We raised hogs and calves for meat. We butchered a calf in the winter and feasted on choice steak and roast until it was gone. We butchered enough hogs to keep us in meat for much of the year, and from them we made lard and soap. We raised chickens, so we had eggs and chickens to eat. Mama sometimes raised turkeys for us to eat at Thanksgiving and Christmas.

For variety, we hunted and killed rabbits, and squirrels to eat. After I was old enough to have a 22 rifle, I learned to be a good shot so I would not waste 22 cartridges. After all they cost a half a cent each. Sometimes Papa, a good shot with a 12-gauge shotgun, went hunting for quail. He usually brought home enough for a meal, and what a feast we would have.

There was no shortage of fish in the river, and in the summertime we caught enough for many good meals.

Our cows kept us in milk products: sweet milk, clabber milk, butter, buttermilk and cottage cheese. We made ice cream in the summertime when we could get 50 cents to buy a 50 pound block of ice. After we finally got a car we hauled ice from town, wrapped in a gunnysack and tied on the bumper.

We hardly realized that times were hard, though the hard times did make a good topic of conversation. We did realize that there was a shortage of money. When we sold our crops in the late fall or early winter, they did not bring much. Animals we sold during the year often did not bring enough to pay the feed bill, but we managed to get by.

To get some spending money when I was a boy, I collected and sold scrap iron in the summertime, and trapped fur-bearing animals in the winter. I also caught fur-bearing animals by hunting with my dogs at night.

Every Saturday, Mama sold some cream and eggs and sometimes a pound of butter she had churned. From these she got enough money to buy the staples at the grocery store. If there was money left over, she saved it against the day she would have to buy me some school clothes, and supplies, and books.

The weekly newspaper told of people out of work in other places, but that did not affect us. We always had plenty of work to do. We met people in town who talked about hard times, about men out of work in other places, and about people standing in bread lines. That was hard for us to understand, for we never had to go hungry. We were just short of money, and that was probably good for us, for it taught us to work hard, to be self-reliant, and to trust in God.

Picking Blackberries

Around the first of July, after crops were laid-by, blackberries ripened in the briar patches on uncultivated hillsides and along creek bottoms. The berries were black, sweet, and juicy. Chiggers were waiting to eat us alive, but we went berry picking anyway.

The June bugs had already discovered the berries and were gorging themselves on the choicest of them. Every so often, while we were busy picking, one of them would take to flight with a sudden buzz, like a small plane taking off. The unexpected sound was always startling.

Before the day of berry picking ended, I always caught one of the largest June bugs to play with after we went home. The June bug looked like a Japanese beetle, though I never heard of a Japanese beetle when I was a boy. The June bug was the same shape and color as the Japanese beetle, but it was more than twice as large. The June bug was not nearly as destructive as its smaller cousin.

I wonder what ever happened to June bugs. I haven't seen one in years. For that matter, what happened to jar flies? They have been almost absent in our part of the country for a number of years. They used to buzz in the trees until you could hardly hear yourself think. It's strange that we have not heard a word about them being an endangered species.

When we got home from blackberry picking, I used to tie a string to one of the back legs of the June bug and released it so it could fly. It would take off, buzzing like a small electric fan. Checked by the thread, he flew around and around, but it couldn't go anywhere. All it could do was buzz! It is easy to see that we didn't have many ways to entertain ourselves in those days.

Remembering how I played with the June bug brings to my mind several random thoughts. Just as I controlled the June bug, the devil has a lot of people on a string, and they can no more free themselves than the June bug could free itself. Like the June bug, they do a lot of buzzing, but they're not going anywhere.

A second thought: only God can make a June bug, and only God can make blackberries for June bugs and for people to eat.

When June bugs are gone, they are gone forever, but when people leave this life, they live on—forever—somewhere. June bugs don't have a choice about their future, but people do. What people do about receiving or rejecting Jesus Christ will determine where they will be in eternity.

Nut Gathering

Another way we coped with hard times was to put up nuts in the fall of the year. Putting up nuts was more fun than working. After the first heavy frost had done its magic, and the trees had put on the colors of fall, it was time to go nut hunting. Most times, Papa, Mama, and I went nut hunting together. We left the house carrying a sack and headed for the big hickory tree, a quarter mile from our house.

Our dogs, as excited as I was, ranged ahead,

and with bounding heart, I ran after them. I did not stop running until I reached the big hickory tree. The dogs soon came to me, out of breath and panting.

The leaves on the hickory tree were lemon yellow. The other trees were bright yellow and gold and rust and brown and red. The nuts on the hickory tree had brown shells. Some nuts had fallen to the grown and lay half hidden in fallen leaves. Some of the shells had burst open.

I ran through the leaves and sent them flying with my feet. I pushed the nuts out of the way, piled up a great pile of leaves, fell in them and rolled in them. The dogs came to lie in the leaves, stretched full-length and panted happily.

When Mama and Papa arrived, we set to work picking up the fallen nuts, shelling them, and putting them in the sack. After we had picked up all the nuts we could find, Papa climbed the tree and shook off all that were loose. Then he climbed down and helped Mama and me finish filling the sack.

When we finished, Papa threw the sack across his shoulder, and we went home. We put the nuts in a dry place to cure, thankful that they had cost us nothing. We did not even have to pay tax on them or pay for gas to go after them.

Usually we did not bring the nuts out until the

week before Thanksgiving. Then, one night after supper, we all sat in the kitchen and cracked nuts and picked out enough kernels to make a hickory nut cake and my favorite dish, chocolate pudding with hickory nuts and raisins in it.

Mama usually baked the nut cake a day or two before Thanksgiving. While it was baking, she would not allow anyone to walk in the kitchen for fear the cake would fall (would not rise properly). The baking cake would fill the house with a delicious aroma. Mama usually cooked my favorite pudding on Thanksgiving morning.

On Thanksgiving Day, we all arose early, and Mama cooked breakfast. We ate hurriedly, then Papa and I went to the barn to feed the mules and milk the cows. When we returned to the house, Mama would send me to the woodpile to get a load of wood for the grate and the kitchen range. Then I would go to the spring and carry water to the house by the bucket load. By the time I finished bringing in the water, the kitchen was warmed by the fire in the range, and Mama was mixing, stirring, preparing a half dozen dishes, and making bread.

Meanwhile, Papa would go out and catch a big turkey gobbler or rooster to be dressed and made ready for the oven.

Soon the house was filled with the wondrous

aroma of cooking food. I will never forget those smells. Nor will I ever forget the food and the time at the table on Thanksgiving Day. That was a great time to be thankful and to enjoy the food. We had so much to eat for Thanksgiving, it made us forget that times were hard.

Chapter 6

Making My Own Toys

Because of the shortage of money my parents and grandparents gave me few store-bought toys when I was growing up. About the most they gave me, except at Christmas, was an occasional rubber ball or a spinning top. At Christmas, Mama and Papa did stuff the stocking I hung by the fireplace with candy, nuts, and some small trinkets. And there was always an inexpensive toy or two.

In those days people observed Christmas in honor of the Lord's birth, and they did not give as many gifts as they do today. Even the Christmas programs at school were centered around the birth of Jesus. So I knew what Christmas was about, but that did not keep me from enjoying the few gifts that I received. Much of my excitement at that time may have been because I was young, but not having much the rest of the year contributed to enjoying the few gifts that I received.

Christmas toys usually did not last long, and when they were broken or worn-out, I had to start improvising as I had before. Like many boys of that era, I learned to make my own toys. They were the best anyway, for there was the fun of making them as well as the fun of playing with them.

Making Marbles

I even learned to make my own marbles. Some boys won their marbles by playing "for keeps." I was a good marble shot, and I could easily have won marbles that way, but I knew I would get a whipping if Mama or Papa found out that I did. Besides, I soon developed scruples of my own, and I did not want to do anything dishonest.

The only way I could get marbles, if I did not find them or if someone did not give them to me, was to make them. Making marbles was a tricky business with only mediocre success. Nonetheless, I did make them on some occasions.

To make marbles I got clay from a clay bank near our house. I had to select clay that was just the right consistency and with the right moisture content. I pinched off the proper amount of clay and rolled it between the palms of my hands until it was smooth and round. I repeated the process until I had made as many round balls of clay as I wanted. Then I took them to the grate in the house and placed them in the glowing embers, being careful not to flatten them in the process.

The marbles had to be left in the fire until they baked as hard as bricks. After that I raked them from the fire and let them cool. That was a lot of work for marbles of poor quality, but I played with them until I could get better marbles.

I do not recall owning a football until I was in high school, but there were other kinds of balls. There were baseballs, hard rubber balls, hollow rubber balls with air in them, sponge rubber balls, and homemade string balls. The sponge balls were best for bouncing. The string balls were best for playing baseball.

Making Balls

In those days men's work socks were so woven that they could be unraveled into many yards of string. So when socks wore out, we used to unravel them and roll the string into balls. It took a long time to make a string ball, but the finished product was a good ball. I discovered that if a small, hard rubber ball was used as a core of a string ball, it made a much more lively ball. In school I played baseball many times with string balls.

Making Spinning Toys

Among our most interesting toys were spinning toys. A spinner could easily be made with a large button and a piece of string. The string only had to be laced through the button and tied to form a circle. The button was set spinning, to the delight of any boy, and most girls, by holding the string at each end of the circle and pulling and relaxing it.

I also made spinning tops from empty thread spools. Making that kind of top required more work than making a button spinner, but it made an excellent toy. All that was needed was a large wooden spool and a short piece of soft lumber. Wooden spools were the only kind that were made for thread when I was a boy. Spools that #9 thread came on were the best for making tops.

With a sharp knife, I cut from the rim of the spool toward the center. Using slightly more than half of the spool, I trimmed it to a point. Then I made a peg from the soft lumber, just large enough to force through the hole in the spool. I left the short end of the peg protruding about three-eights of an inch from the sharp end of the spool and sharpened it to a point. I cut the other end of the peg about three quarters of an inch above the top of the spool. That finished the top. I set it spinning by twisting the peg between my thumb and middle finger and dropping it on a smooth surface. The trick was to see how long I could make the top spin.

Spools were also useful for making other toys. They were nice to roll just as they were, and they were good for making a kind of two-wheeled tractor, using a short stick, a rubber band, and a small piece of soap. There is no need for me to tell how I made the tractors, because no boy in his right mind would bother to make such a toy today. But in my day such toys kept active boys occupied for many happy hours.

Making Other Toys

Besides homemade balls, marbles, tops, and tractors, I made and flew kites, and I made popguns from elder limbs, stick horses from short sticks, and cars from sticks and small wheels from broken toy wagons that some other child had discarded. I rode barrel hoops and automobile tires, and I made sleds from scrap lumber so I could go sleigh riding on the snow in the winter.

I made rings to wear, molding them from lead, fashioning them with my pocket knife, and plating them with copper. I even made a toy boat that was propelled by a rubber band. Add to this the bows and arrows, slings, slingshots, deadfall traps, and fishing tackle I made, and you will see that a boy growing up in the Great Depression was not really poor. In fact, I was exceedingly rich. I had the hills and the valleys to play over, and I had the four seasons of the year to give me variety. I knew instinctively what many have never learned in this affluent day. With the little I had, I knew how to play and how to enjoy life.

In that day people did not have to be entertained. They entertained themselves. And teenagers didn't need dope to make them high. They were high with the joy of living and with the thrill of making the most of what they had.

Even the grown-ups knew how to entertain themselves. Often neighbors got together at night to talk, to tell stories, to play parlor games, and to listen to someone play the "banger" or the "gitar."

On Saturdays everybody went to town to sell cream and eggs, and to buy a few groceries, but mostly they went to visit with friends and neighbors. Also on Saturdays, grown-ups sometimes splurged and bought us a nickel bottle of pop or a nickel ice cream cone.

I can never forget my grandmother telling about treating a neighbor woman, who seldom went to town, to her first ice cream cone. When my grandmother had eaten the ice cream off the top and started eating the cone, the lady exclaimed, in some consternation, "Why, Emily, do you eat the box?"

Some people think of "The good old days" as days of hardships. Times were hard, and those of us who lived through them have not forgotten. We had to work hard, and we had little money to buy the things we wanted. Yet, in spite of the hardships, we enjoyed life in a way people of today cannot understand. Call it nostalgia if you wish, but we often long for the quieter, simpler time we knew in the years gone by.

Chapter 7

The Way Things Used to Be

When I was growing up it was almost as cold in our house in the wintertime as it was outdoors. The only way we could get warm was to huddle around the fireplace and turn ourselves from time to time to warm both our front and backsides. At mealtime we often filled our plates and carried them to our chairs by the fireplace so we could eat with some small degree of comfort.

When we got in bed at night, the sheets were like ice. I spent countless nights shivering on those cold sheets with my knees drawn up toward my chin until the bed finally began to get warm. Then slowly, inch by inch, I moved my toes toward the foot of the bed. On especially cold nights, I used to get under the featherbed and sleep on the straw tick. The cold could not reach me there, so I soon drifted into dreamland.

The next morning about four o'clock, Papa would call, "Louis Walker, get up and build a fire."

I dreaded the cold, and for a moment I lay there debating whether I should dress first or build the fire first. If I built the fire first, the cold would go through my nightclothes as if I were outdoors. If I dressed first, the garments I put on would be like ice to my bare skin.

Our boxed house had been weatherboarded, but there were still cracks in the wall, and the icy wind blew through them with impunity. Often it left a dusting of snow on my bed.

There was no underpinning under our house, and the wind swept under it. There was no sub floor, so the cold easily penetrated the three-quarter inch pine floor. Wind even came up through the cracks. When I got out of bed the linoleum that covered the floor was as cold as the ice on the creek.

After I got the fire burning in the grate, I would go to the kitchen and start a fire in the cook stove. The water in the water bucket had frozen solid during the night, so I would put it on the stove to thaw. Then I would go back to the fire I had built in the grate and huddled near it until the room began to warm.

What a blessed day it was when Papa finally

bought a Warm Morning Heater and put it in the middle bedroom. That big heating stove made the house warmer in winter than it had ever been, and, when we banked the fire before going to bed, the house did not get unbearably cold during the night. All I had to do the next morning was to shake out the ashes and put in a fresh supply of coal.

A Changing World

It was a far different world when we did not have central heat, indoor plumbing, a victrola, electric lights, a radio, a TV, a VCR, or even a phone. I remember when we did not have a washing machine, a refrigerator, or any of the other electrical gadgets we take for granted today. We never thought we were deprived, though we did spend hours looking at the Sears and Roebuck, and Montgomery Ward catalogs, and dreaming of the things we would buy when we got the money.

Things We Did Have

We had time together as a family, and we had friends, neighbors, and kinfolk who took time to visit us from time to time. If they stayed away until we grew lonely for them, we visited them. We had love to spare. We had our dreams, and we took time to play, to fish and to hunt. We had a Bible, and we read it. We had a few good books, among them was, *Pilgrim's Progress, The Christian's Secret of a Happy Life,* and a book of Longfellow's poems.

For entertainment, we had a stereoscope and a few pictures for it. I spent many happy hours viewing those pictures over and over. When I was a good-sized boy, Mama bought a second-hand box camera. My what fun we had making pictures with it. Mama managed to buy film, and we made pictures on every occasion. The pictures were black and white, of course, but that did not matter. We thought our camera made better pictures than any other camera in the county.

Our New Washing Machine

I will never forget the day a salesman came to our house and convinced Mama to let him demonstrate a new patented washing machine. Anything would be better than boiling our clothes outside in the double boiler, over an open fire and washing them in a tub with a washboard. So she agreed to let him demonstrate his machine.

Even if we didn't buy it, she reasoned, he would do a week's washing for us, but I would still have to carry water from the creek at the bottom of the hill.

We were so excited at the prospect of seeing how the new washer worked, I carried water and filled all the tubs we had before the salesman arrived. Mama brought out all our dirty clothes, sorted them, and put them in separate piles.

When the salesman arrived, we watched him bring in a contraption that looked like anything but a washing machine. Folded up, it stood about as tall as I was, and it was about 30 inches across. It was made of strips of wood that were held together by metal parts. There was a large crank near the top that was attached to some cogs that drove two white rubber rollers.

The man lifted some screen door latches and folded down legs on each side of the contraption. They formed a platform for large washtubs on each side of the upright piece. He brought in two large wooden tubs and a corrugated, wooden roller with some smaller, round, spring-loaded, rollers attached to it. He set the tubs on the platforms, one on each side, and put the roller assembly in place in one of them. The assembly hooked on the upright piece and rested in the tub. I know this is complicated, but it is the only way I know how to describe the machine.

The salesman had me to pour hot water in the tub with the assembly in it. He put in soap and started demonstrating how the machine worked. It was exciting to watch him crank the clothes back and forth through the rollers until they were clean, then crank them through the ringer assembly to remove excess water from them. That certainly beat ringing clothes by hand.

Mama decided that the machine beat washing the old way all to pieces, so she persuaded Papa to let her buy it.

After we got the new machine, it still took a full day for me and Mama to do a week's washing, but it was easier than washing in the old way.

Not long after we bought our washing machine, our neighbor bought a new gasoline-powered washing machine. They kept it on their back porch so the fumes would not poison them while they were washing. Each time they washed, we could hear the motor of that machine popping as it ran. Perhaps we took comfort that our machine was not as noisy as theirs, that it did not make fumes that could poison us, and we did not have to buy gasoline for it.

Our First Telephone

It was especially exciting when we finally got a telephone. Several of our neighbors had phones long before we did, but Papa finally broke down and had one installed in our house.

I will never forget the day when two men came to install our phone. Much had already been done to make it possible for us to get a phone, but it still was quite involved to get it installed in our house.

Big poles, with many telephone lines, had long since been set along the main roads, and smaller poles, with only two lines, had been set along our road. The big poles, with their strands of wire, added considerably to the scenery along the main roads. I find it nostalgic that they are now gone forever. Present and future generations will never see their like.

Those telephone poles looked like tall crosses with two relatively short crossbars. Each crossbar had wooden, threaded dowels fastened vertically along its top edge, four or five inches apart. A green glass insulator was screwed onto each dowel. Gray uninsulated wires, perhaps #10 gauge, were strung from pole to pole like the strings of great harps. The wires were stretched tight, and in cold weather they were said to sing. Many times I have heard the off key, minor humming of the telephone wires.

The poles along our road did not have crossbars. They had two dowels with green insulators nailed near the top of them. They carried the wires that made it possible for us to have a phone. The lines along our road did not sing, but they carried many a conversation.

The phone company had set poles across our

property to our house before they came to install the phone. These poles had only one glass insulator to carry a single strand of wire.

I had a natural bent toward all things mechanical or electrical, so when the men came to install our telephone, I watched them with great interest.

One of the men asked Mama where she wanted the phone, and she pointed to a place near the mantle on our front room wall. The other man went out to their truck and brought in the telephone. It was in a large oak case with a transmitter mounted on an iron extension from the front. There was an oak shelf below. Near the top of the case was a pair of round ringers, like the one on top of an alarm clock. A crank was mounted on the right side of the case, and a hook to hang the receiver on was mounted on the left side. All the metal parts were painted black. The telephone was not pretty by today's standards, but we thought it was a seven-day wonder.

One of the men drove a copper rod in the ground near the front step. He connected one of a twisted pair of wires to the ground post and the other one to the telephone line. He ran the twisted wires along the porch ceiling, through the outside wall of the house, and along the wall of the front room to the phone. The other man brought in two large dry-cell batteries, put them in the phone case, and connected them.

I watched, hardly believing, when he picked up the receiver and turned the crank. The bell on the front of the case rang, and a moment later he started talking to the operator in Lancaster, five miles away.

The man explained to us that we were on a party line with several other families. Each family had a different ring. A single short ring would get one family. Two short rings would get another family. One family's ring was three shorts. Another family's ring was three longs. Besides those rings, there was a short and a long, a long and a short, and so on. Our ring was two longs and a short.

We could call people on our party line by simply ringing their ring with the crank. When we wanted someone who was not on our line, we had to ring the operator in Lancaster. Her ring was a single long ring. When she answered, "Operator," we had to give her the number of the party we wanted. She would plug us into the line we wanted with a patch cord and ring the number we had given her. They left us a small phone book containing all the numbers of people in the county.

After the telephone man left, we looked at the phone for a moment. Then Mama looked at the paper she had written the different rings for our neighbors on and rang the nearest neighbor. A moment later they were talking. We had arrived. We had a telephone.

I soon looked inside the phone case and saw that the crank turned an armature inside some large horseshoe magnets. I knew that turning a wire-wound armature inside a magnetic field generated an electric current. That was what made the phones along the lines ring when the crank was turned, I realized.

I knew that if a person touched a wire that was carrying an electric current it would shock them, so I tried an experiment. I climbed a ladder and tied a piece of copper wire to the telephone wire that ran from our house. Then I climbed down, stood on the moist ground, and held the wire, waiting for someone to make a call. Soon somebody made a call, and I felt my arms tingling and shaking like someone had them in a tight grip and was shaking them. I couldn't decide whether it hurt or tickled. Altogether it was not an unpleasant feeling, and for some days I held to that wire every time I had a chance, waiting to get shocked again. I strongly advise that no one try such an experiment today. The currents we use these days are far too strong to play with. Touching a live electric wire can be fatal.

I suppose the telephone and the patented washing machine spoiled us. After we got them, we were always wanting something new.

Things Do Not Satisfy

When I was in grade school, I remember being made to memorize the phrase, "There is no end to human wants and desires." Alas, how true that is. When a person gets something new, they soon want something else.

Material things are nice to have, but they do not satisfy. Being saved and living for God is the only thing that does satisfy. God tells us, ". . . *godliness with contentment is great gain" (1 Tim. 6:6).*

All too often we become slaves to the things we have. We often get so many things, it takes all our time to clean, store, and keep them in repair, and we have little time to enjoy them. In the process, we often lose the things that really matter. Our family had had so little for so long, only the shortage of money kept us from buying more than we really needed.

Chapter 8

Work and Relaxation

Papa and I worked long and hard to make a living on our little farm. I especially remember chopping weeds out of the cornfield in the hot weather of early July. The corn was over our heads, and not the slightest breeze could reach us. The temperature outside the field was usually in the upper nineties, and, with the hot sun shining down on us, the temperature in the cornfield was well over a hundred. Chopping weeds out of the corn was hard work, and we perspired freely. Sweat bees buzzed around us and stung us from time to time. The ground was dry, and dust fogged up and stuck to our sweat-moistened bodies.

Call to Dinner

Our days in the fields started early, and it seemed that dinnertime would never come, but we had a way of knowing when it did. A passenger train passed through Hyattsville, two miles away, at 11:30 each morning. The engineer always blew the whistle at the road crossing, and that was our signal that it was dinnertime.

On days when we were plowing Ol' Jack, one of our work mules, hitched to the double-shovel plow, it was easy to tell when noontime was approaching, even before we heard the train. About fifteen minutes before time for the train, Ol' Jack would start listening for it. With his big ears, he always heard it long before we did, and when the engineer blew the whistle at the crossing, there was no holding him. He knew we would stop for dinner at the end of the row, and he lost no time getting there.

When we were not working Ol' Jack, Papa and I listened for the train. When we heard it, Papa always insisted that we work on to the end of the row before we stopped for dinner, and, like Ol' Jack, I certainly worked fast until we got there.

Mama always had dinner on the table in the kitchen when we reached the house. She too had heard the train and had hurried to have everything ready when we arrived.

Mama cooked dinner on our coal-burning

stove, and the temperature in the kitchen was
even higher than it was in the cornfield. We seldom complained about the heat, for Mama had
worked hard cooking dinner in the hot kitchen,
and she was not complaining.

Mama often dressed and fried a chicken, gathered vegetables from our garden and cooked
them, and made biscuits and baked them in the
oven. If the ice we had bought in town on Saturday had not all been used or melted, she brewed
tea. The amber liquid sparkled, and the ice
tinkled in the glasses.

We had the luxury of a short rest after dinner. Then we went back to the field and worked
until the sun was going down. That was our signal to go to the barn and take the harness off Ol'
Jack, if we had worked him. After that we fed
the animals, milked the cows, gathered the eggs,
and carried water and coal to the house. Long
before we finished, Mama had an oil lamp burning in the kitchen, and we knew that she would
soon have supper on the table.

A Swim After Supper

We ate supper by the light of the oil lamp in
a house that was still as hot as a blast furnace.
After supper, I often asked permission to go for
a swim in the concrete tank on a neighbor's farm
at the foot of our hill. Sometimes Papa went with
me. After our swim we returned to the house and

changed clothes. Then Papa and I usually went out to the front yard and laid down on the grass, and Mama would sit on the front porch, not far away.

Looking Up At the Stars

Papa and I looked up at the stars and often started talking about them. We wondered how many there were and how far away they were. Sometimes we would locate the Big Dipper, the Little Dipper, and the North Star. Those were the only stars we knew by name.

We often saw "falling stars," and talked about them. If we saw several falling stars in one night, Mama would wonder aloud if that could be a sign of the coming of the Lord. We did not know, but it was something to think about—and talk about.

After a while a cool breeze would fan our bodies, and we would go inside and go to bed. We slept with our doors and windows open to let in as much air as possible. There was almost no crime in our neighborhood, so we did not worry about someone coming in the house to kill or rob us. Our only thought was to get a good night's sleep.

Time to Relax

There were times when work was less pressing, and we had time to sit in the swing on the front porch to rest and talk. We breathed fresh, country air and felt a gentle breeze fan our cheeks, as we watched the world go by. That beat watching TV by a hundred miles. What we saw from our front porch was real. Most of what people see on TV is make-believe. Even much of the news is contrived, slanted, and doctored to fit a particular point-of-view—usually not our point- of-view. People watch a make-believe world on TV and breathe air that has been cooled by an air conditioner.

While we were sitting on our porch old friends sometimes passed in a horse and buggy and waved. We would wave back and wonder aloud where they were going.

From time to time a friend would stop to pass the time of day, and we would catch up on the latest neighborhood news, sports and weather.

We would learn that there had been a good rain in the next county, though it was still dry in our locality. We would learn what was in the local paper this week, and what the outcome of the high school football game against a rival team had been last Friday. That kind of sports news meant a lot more than who won a tennis match in England. The report on the weather in the lower end of the county meant more than hearing what the weather was like in Alaska. And news of a shooting in the next county last Saturday night meant more than hearing what is happening in Namibia or some other far away place. There was personal news, like how Aunt Susie was feeling since her fall and how the new calf that was born last week was doing.

A passerby, who was driving a car, might also pull to the roadside and stop to talk. He might even get out and go with us to see our garden. If he did, we would load him down with summer squash, tomatoes, and cucumbers when he left. After the visitor was gone, the pastor of the church just might stop by and be invited to sit on the porch with us.

After catching up on news about our family and the near neighbors, the pastor would read to us from the Bible and offer prayer. Then, after being loaded down with fresh eggs and vegetables, he would excuse himself and go on his way, leaving us in a happy frame of mind. No doubt about it, the old front porch was far ahead of TV, and it served us well in the days when I was growing up.

Sitting By the Fire

The front porch was only good for sitting on in the summertime. When cold weather came, our sitting had to be moved to chairs before the fireplace. We gained a lot of comfort when we installed central heating in our homes, but we lost something very valuable. Before we had central heat, cold weather brought families together around an old-fashioned fireplace. Families used to spend countless hours around the fire, and they had time to talk, to share, to play games, to read, and to entertain themselves, and each other. Being forced to sit close together, they got to know each other better. Neighbors often came to sit before the fire, and we got to know them better too. In front of the fire, we exchanged news and discussed problems. Often we shared our burdens, and the time around the fireplace made us better neighbors.

Sitting before the fire alone, can also be a healing experience. King David wrote in Psalm 39:3, *". . . while I was musing the fire burned . . ."* David's heart was hot within him as he sat before the fire. Afterward he cried in verse 4, *"Lord, make me to know mine end, and the measure of my days, what it is; that I may know how frail I am."*

In my mind's eye I can still see the smoke curling upward in the grate, dancing, white and gray, dying almost away, then rising again. I can almost see the amber fire, slowly burning a blackened log, and glowing embers, and sparks flying upward when someone punched the fire with a poker.

Who can forget the old family altar before the fireplace? When bedtime drew near, the old family Bible was brought out. The older members of the family became quiet, and the younger ones were made to stop teasing each other and giggling. A chapter was read from the Bible, usually by the father, sometimes by the mother. After that, each member of the family would arise, push their chairs back and kneel before them. Prayers were offered, then good nights were said, and, by the light of a kerosene lamp, they went to their rooms and to bed.

Central heating made it possible for family members to scatter all over the house, and the close contact around the fireplace was gone forever. Central heating gave family members more time to themselves and less time for each other.

Television has, to a degree, brought families together again, but it's not the same. Now people sit in their nice, warm family rooms and watch talking pictures on a screen. They no longer entertain each other, nor do they share information with each other. Instead, they listen to news from halfway around the world.

These days it's not even necessary to think or to ask a loved one what they think. The TV people tell us what to think. In many homes there

is no time for the family altar these days. Someone might miss the late show. Maybe the people
who talk about the good old days have a point.

The Rainy Days

In spite of all the work we had to do when I
was growing up, we still found time for fun and
games. Often we got a break on a rainy day, especially in the springtime. A sudden spring rain
usually brought a break from work and allowed
me time to play.

We had no weather forecast when I was growing up, except what was written in *The Farmer's
Almanac.* We didn't fully trust what it said, except when it was time to plant something or to
wean a calf. Then we wanted to know if the sign
was right.

Rains often came unexpectedly, and we
would be caught in the field. When the rain began to fall Papa hoped it would stop, and we
could continue to work. Only when it started
raining harder did we drop our hoes where we
were and run to the shelter of the nearest tree. If
the rain did not soon stop, the leaves on the tree
would start dripping water, and we would have
to run to the barn for shelter.

After we got to the barn, Papa would stand
near the open door, looking out and wishing the
rain would stop, and I would look around for a

way to entertain myself. Sometimes, if the rain continued, some neighbor boys, wearing raincoats and hats, would come to the barn. One of them would suggest a marble game and bring out a bag of marbles he had in his pocket. We would sweep the dust from a place in the middle of the driveway and draw a ring on the ground for the game. Then we would set the marbles in place, choose our taws, and start the game. We passed the time on many a rainy day in that way.

We Entertained Ourselves

When we had some free time on days when it was not raining, we played horseshoes or baseball. Sometimes the grown-ups joined us in a game of croquet. After we got a victrola, neighbors often came at night to visit and to listen to the records we had.

Before we owned an automobile, about all the traveling we did was to town, or to the home of my maternal grandparents, or to the river to go fishing. All the travel we did on horseback or in a buckboard (a buggy with the top removed).

Fishing in the River

On Saturday afternoons during the summer, Papa and I often went to Dix River to fish. He did most of the fishing, graveling under rocks with his hands for catfish. While Papa fished, I spent most of the time playing in the river.

Humorous things sometimes happened when we went fishing. I remember a time when Papa and a neighbor, named Bill, were fishing together in the river. They found a large catfish under a submerged rock. They had to dive to reach the opening under the rock. Papa and Bill both wanted to catch that fish, and each was determined to beat the other to it. I have no idea why, but Bill was wearing a large felt hat as he fished. He didn't want to get his hat wet, so he took it off and put it on Papa's head. Paying no heed to the hat, Papa dived at the same moment that Bill did. As both men disappeared beneath the water, Bill's big hat floated off Papa's head, and the current caught it and carried it down the river. It was really comical to see the hat floating away with neither man in sight.

A Thanksgiving Blizzard

In the fall and winter we hunted, both for entertainment and for food. Strong in my memory ing, I went home to visit my parents and to go rabbit hunting. One of my deacons and his family went with me. I was excited that I was going to see Mama and Papa, and that we could put our feet under Mama's table and enjoy the good dinner she was sure to have. I was also excited to have my deacon and his family with me, and, of course, I was excited about going hunting in the old neighborhood. There were always plenty of rabbits on our farm and on adjoining farms, so I assured my deacon that we would have a great day of hunting.

Soon after we arrived, Papa, my deacon, and I left the house to go hunting. We were glad to be out of doors, and I imagine the women were glad to have us out of the way while they were finishing the Thanksgiving dinner.

When we left the house the sun was shining, and it was so warm it seemed more like early September than late November. But the good weather did not last. We had gone only a short distance when a cold wind started blowing, and clouds started scudding across the sky. We buttoned our coats and continued on our way, expecting no more than a mild change in the weather. But we soon learned that a real winter storm was in the making. The temperature plummeted, and snow started falling from the overcast sky.

That day I observed one of the strangest things I have ever seen in nature. We came upon a large snake in the open, almost paralyzed by the cold. It had no business being out that late in the season, and it certainly had no business being out in the weather we were experiencing. It had been so warm in the early part of the day, the snake had crawled from its place of hibernation. Then the temperature had dropped so suddenly, it had not been able to crawl back to a place of safety.

Never have I seen the weather change more rapidly or more drastically than it did that day. I do not remember killing any rabbits, but I do remember that the metal parts of my gun became as cold as ice. My hands ached in spite of the gloves I was wearing.

The wind continued to blow, and a heavy snow started coming down, so we decided to give up the hunt and return to the house. On our way we struggled against a blasting wind with an arctic breath, and a slanting wall of falling snow made it difficult for us to find our way.

Oh how good the house looked when we finally saw it. And it was wonderful to get inside and smell roasting turkey, pungent spices, and a variety of cooking food. Dinner was well under way, and we were glad, for we were hungry after our walk in the cold.

When dinner was ready, we sat down around the table, now in the dining room, a recent improvement. We enjoyed ham and turkey with dressing and cranberries and a great variety of vegetables, jello, chocolate pudding, and, of course, Mama's specialty, hickory nut cake. What a time we had feasting and visiting. We hardly noticed that the wind was shaking the house, and that the snow was continuing to fall.

Too soon the short winter day was drawing to a close, and we knew that we should be going home. I opened the door and looked out, and a blast of wind nearly wrenched the doorknob from my hand. I had a glimpse of snow, piled deep and drifting, and I forced the door closed, convinced that the roads were now impassable. There was nothing to do but spend the night.

Soon my deacon and I braved the storm with Papa and helped him feed and milk. The wind had grown colder. Even in the barn the cold was numbing, so we did the chores in record time.

When we finished, we fought our way back to the house, carrying a bucket of milk and some eggs we had gathered. We went out again and carried in water from the cistern and coal from the snow-covered coal pile.

We enjoyed leftovers for supper, then sat around the fireplace in the living room to soak up heat and talk. When bedtime came, it was good to get in bed and feel the warmth of a featherbed, but I could not help worrying about the ordeal of going home the next day.

It would be difficult to start the car after it had been in the cold all day and all night. After we got it started, we would have to shovel snow away from the wheels. We would probably have to harness the mules and pull the car until we reached the graveled road. Even then, it was possible that the car would get stuck in the snow, and we would have to jack up the back wheels, get down on our knees in the snow and put chains on the tires.

I do not remember the details of the journey home. It was likely the way I had envisioned it while lying there in the featherbed.

My father and mother have long been gone to Heaven, so I can no longer visit them, but I am glad that I can relive in memory that snow-filled Thanksgiving Day of long ago.

Chapter 9

My Most Embarrassing Moments

I grew up at the end of the road and the head of the creek. My parents were timid, and I grew up as timid as they were. It is likely that the isolation of our home also contributed to my timidity. It is a miracle that I ever got over being timid.

I had little contact with other children until my family moved when I was six to the farm where I grew up. Our nearest neighbor, a quarter mile away, had a little girl about my age. We became playmates and played together occasionally.

Within a year or two her family moved away, and a new family moved into the house they had vacated. They had a large family, and some of their boys were about my age. I played with them when I could, but my contact with them did not get me over my timidity.

Being timid and self-conscious caused me to commit some embarrassing blunders in my early years.

A Broken Bed Rail

About the time I was old enough to begin to be attracted to girls, I visited in the home of a boy who had two or three sisters. Some other young people were visiting there also. The family had no living room, so in the afternoon we all wandered into the bedroom of the parents and sat down on the side of the bed to look at some pictures.

Shortly one of the boys poked me in the ribs. I jumped and landed back on the bed. There was a loud cracking sound, as the bed rail split from end to end and the bed crashed to the floor. I was so mortified, I left at once. I doubt that I ever set foot in that house again.

A Table Blunder

Another most embarrassing moment occurred in the home of the barber who had been cutting my hair for several months at the going price of 35 cents. We became friends, and one afternoon after he closed his shop he invited me to his home. When I arrived, he introduced me to his wife, an attractive, neatly dressed, apparently well educated young woman. I was ill-at-ease from the moment I saw her.

She soon brought out some berries and cream and some cookies, and put them on a small table. Then she invited me and her husband to come to the table and partake of her refreshments. Despite my timidity, I managed to eat my bowl of berries and the cookies without mishap. Then I made a most embarrassing blunder.

At home I had developed a bad habit. No one told me it was a bad habit, so I continued to do it until it became second nature. Where I ate at the table, my chair was near the wall, and I had a habit of tilting my chair against the wall after I finished eating. So, when I finished eating my bowl of berries I tilted my chair back as I always did at home. But there was no wall behind me. So my chair kept going, and on its way down, it struck a floor lamp and knocked it over. The power cord tangled around my arm. My feet went up under the tabletop, and the table started rising like a hot-air balloon.

Dishes rattled and started sliding across the table. I knew that everything on the table was going to crash to the floor, that the pretty china was going to be broken, and that cream and berry juice were going to spill all over the expensive rug, but the barber saved the day. He instantly put both hands on top of the table and pressed down. That kept the table from upsetting, but it didn't keep me from landing on the floor.

Embarrassed beyond words, I crawled from under the table, disentangled the electric cord from around my arm, and set the floor lamp upright. My friend's quick action saved the china, but it did nothing for my bruised feelings. I soon excused myself and left. My barber friend never invited me to his home again.

The Day I Lost Control

I will never forget the day I almost lost my sermon. During the first summer of my ministry, I was holding a meeting in a one-roomed schoolhouse in a community where there was no church. In this school, as in other schools in that day, the teacher taught several grades in one room. There were children of all ages and sizes in the room, so they had desks of varying sizes. The largest desks were in the back of the room and the smallest ones were in the front, near the teacher's desk.

I was a young, single preacher, and many young people attended the meeting. Some of the girls sat near the front, so they would be near the preacher I suppose. One young lady, who was large for her age and decidedly overweight, came down front and sat at a tiny desk that was designed for a child in the first grade. The desks in those days were made with the desktop fastened to the back of the seat. The desk in front of a pupil was part of the next seat. These desks were fastened to the floor with not much room between the seat and the desktop.

This large girl poured herself into one of the tiny seats. She filled all the space between the seat and the desktop, and she overflowed into all the space around it. It looked as if the seat was not there, and the desktop was smothered under her big arms.

I paid no attention to her until she got tickled at something I said. I have no memory of what I said that tickled her, but I have never forgotten how she reacted. She turned her head back and opened her mouth wide enough to swallow a large biscuit without chewing it, and started laughing. She laughed until the windows rattled, and she beat on the little desk with her big hands until it creaked. I thought she would break it into splinters. I got tickled at her, and laughed. Everyone in the room started laughing, and there was no way to stop them.

I tried to go on with my sermon. I turned my eyes toward the ceiling so I would no longer see the girl, but I could not forget her. Every time I opened my mouth to say something, I broke out laughing again. I doubt that the service that day did anything for anyone else, but it did a lot for me. It taught me the value of having my emotions under control.

The Broken Lampshade

Another most embarrassing event occurred soon after I became pastor of two half-time churches, Mitchellsburg Baptist Church in Mitchellsburg, Kentucky, and Salem Baptist Church, three miles over the knob from Mitchellsburg. I was a timid, inexperienced country boy, and this was my first experience as a pastor. I needed the rough edges knocked off of me, and the Lord knew how to do it. I think He let some things happen just for that reason.

Salem Baptist Church had a typical, one-roomed, frame church building with only one door. All the Sunday school classes met in that one room without even curtains to separate them. There was no plumbing and no electricity. So there were no electric lights. Air-conditioning had not been invented, and furnace heat was rare.

Salem Baptist Church was hot in the summertime and cold in the winter. In summer the people tried to cool themselves with hand-held fans the undertaker had given to the church so if any of them died, their family would know who to call. In the winter the people huddled around a pot-bellied stove near the center of the room.

At night, summer and winter, they squinted at songbooks by the light of coal oil (kerosene) lamps that were mounted along the walls. Shiny reflectors behind the lamps made them give a little more light, but they still did a poor job of lighting the building.

The people at Salem loved the Lord, and perhaps they were as excited to have me for their pastor as I was to be their pastor. But they could not have been more ill-at-ease than I was.

The first Sunday night I preached for them, it troubled me that the church was so poorly lighted. The new Aladdin kerosene lamps had come on the market not long before that. People who had no electricity thought the Aladdin Lamp was the greatest thing since the invention of the wheel. It was the greatest improvement in oil lamps since the time of Abraham. In his day, and in the days when Jesus was on earth, an oil lamp was a small container of oil with a wick. The first improvement on the oil lamps was when someone figured out how to put a glass chimney over the flame. That was the kind of lights we used when I was a boy. Then came the marvelous Aladdin Lamp, with a mantle that contained the flame so that it made the mantle glow. That kind of lamp was much brighter than the old-fashioned lamps. I decided right away that Salem Baptist Church had to have an Aladdin Lamp.

I never thought to ask the church to buy a

lamp. Instead, I bought one out of my meager funds. The Aladdin Lamp I bought had a glass shade and a chain so it could be hung from the ceiling.

The next Sunday that I preached at Salem, I proudly gave the lamp to the church. The men of the church hung it that afternoon, and that night there was light in the old church building such as had never been before.

I only preached at Salem every other Sunday, so before I returned to preach again the oil in the lamp had to be replenished. Whoever put the oil in the lamp must have decided that the glass shade wasn't worth the trouble it took to remove it and replace it so, instead of putting it back on the lamp, they placed it in the middle of the bench behind the pulpit.

On my next appointed Sunday, I returned to Salem to preach (officiate might be a better word). I was all the staff the church had, so I had to lead the singing, make the announcements, call for the deacons to receive the offering, pray over it, and preach.

Remember that I was inexperienced and that I was half scared to death when I was in the pulpit. I didn't know what to do with my hands or with the rest of me for that matter. I sometimes stood behind the pulpit desk. Often I moved from side to side, or walked back and forth across the platform. Sometimes, for no reason at all, I would set down on the bench behind the pulpit stand.

That Sunday, about the middle of the third song, I backed up and sat down on the glass shade, and pandemonium followed. The shade didn't crash. It exploded! I jumped straight up in the air and landed in the midst of the broken glass that had scattered all over the pulpit. The day was ruined for me. I was embarrassed and humiliated beyond words. I couldn't walk for the glass on the floor, so for once I stood in one place and preached. How I ever got through that sermon, I will never know.

I'm sure the people did not soon forget what happened that day, and I have certainly never forgotten it. The memory now causes me to smile, but it was no laughing matter when it happened. I'm sure that this experience, and others like it, helped to prepare me for hard knocks I would have later in my ministry.

Embarrassed Church Members

The time came when an embarrassing situation troubled other people more than it did me, for I had learned to shrug off such events and go on as though they had not happened.

After I had become well-known as a radio preacher, I was invited to hold a revival in a good-sized country church near Berea, Kentucky. The church did not have a pastor at the time, so the deacons were in charge. They must have thought I was a big-shot preacher, for they were on pins and needles. They had everything planned down to a T. They received an offering every night, and they gave it to me in cash. I think they must have agreed how much each person would give each night, for the offering was always the same amount. Just an example of how they wanted things to go.

Above the pulpit desk in that church, there was a hanging lamp of ancient vintage. It had once been an oil-burning lamp, but it had been electrified. It was a curious looking lamp, with a clear bowl for oil, and with two burners, with glass chimneys, going off at 45 degree angles. The bowl was filled with a good quantity of water, I suppose to make it look as if it had oil in it

That lamp must have been hanging there since the flood, but one night, just as I stepped forward and laid my open Bible on the desk, it fell. It struck the desk, and the bowl and chimneys broke. Water from the bowl wet my Bible, and nearly drowned me, and shattered glass went everywhere.

Women rushed to the pulpit and started mopping up the water with a tablecloth, or something they had miraculously gotten from somewhere. Men came and started picking up pieces of glass as if they were collecting diamonds. Somebody blotted the water off my Bible, and someone tried to brush the water off the front of my coat, tie, and shirt.

I told the people it was all right, that I suppose that lamp had to fall sometime, and now was as good a time as any. Really, I don't remember all I said, but I shrugged off the event and went on with the service. By that time I was case hardened to such incidents, but the people of that church were not. They were so mortified, I doubt that they heard anything I said that night.

Chapter 10

Molding Influences

When I was a baby my mother carried me to the church across the road from where I was born. She wanted to make sure nothing was lacking in my upbringing, but in future years it was not always possible for her to keep me in church.

My Years Out of Church

My father soon gave up blacksmithing and moved to a farm on a back road, too far from a church for Mama to attend. A year or two later, they moved again. This time they settled on a good road, but again there was no church nearby. Having no way to travel except on horseback, Mama did not attend church while we lived there.

The Move to County Pike

Our next move was to a farm on the County

Pike in Garrard County, where I finished growing up.

Again, there was no church near enough for Mama to attend, but in the summertime there was Sunday school on Sunday afternoons at Hyattsville, two miles from where we lived. She took me there to Sunday school when I was so small my feet did not touch the floor when I sat on the homemade pews. That is my first memory of attending a religious service of any kind.

I recall little of what I was taught in Sunday school, but I remember the beautiful cards they passed out each Sunday. I treasured them even more than the bird pictures I got out of Arm & Hammer baking soda boxes each time my mother opened a box.

The Sunday school cards were not as pretty as the bird pictures, but they had words on the back, and, before I was old enough to read, Mama used to read them to me each Sunday after we got home.

My Conversion

When I was about eleven years old, a preacher and a singer came to our neighborhood and got permission to hold a revival in the Sunday school building. They stayed at our house during the meeting, and we rode to church with them every night in the preacher's car. Mama and Papa agreed that the preacher couldn't preach very well, but they thought the singer was all right.

I remember hearing the preacher and the singer practice singing at our house. One of their songs was *No Disappointment In Heaven.* I had never heard the song before, and I thought it was beautiful.

The meeting lasted two weeks, and I was the only one converted in the meeting. That put me in good company. Dr. B. R. Lakin and Dr. George Truett were the only converts in revivals they attended when they were boys.

I'm not sure the preaching had any effect on me, but one night during the invitation a neighbor lady asked me if I didn't want to be saved. I told her I didn't know. She whispered that my mother was praying for me. I looked across the aisle and saw that my mother's lips were moving in prayer. That was all it took. I went forward and knelt at an old wooden bench at the front of the building and received Jesus as my Savior.

I slept that night with a new peace in my heart, and the next morning, as I walked the graveled road to school, I felt as if I were walking on air. As I drew near the country schoolhouse , someone shouted, "Hello, sanctified." That was my first taste of persecution. It made my heart ache, but it did not keep me from being glad that I was a Christian.

My Early Life as a Christian

For a time I was the only Christian in my school, but the school was not entirely without Christian influence. We always sang a song or two before starting our lessons, and the teacher always read a passage from the Bible and had us to recite the Lord's Prayer. How sad that teachers are not allowed to do that in our schools today.

After I was saved my parents started driving our horse and buggy to church in Lancaster, five miles away. We attended faithfully for a year or two. Those were the happiest days of my boyhood. I still remember sitting in the pew during church each Sunday morning and putting a nickel, contributed by my parents, in an envelope and placing it in the collection plate. I loved my pastor, and to this day I treasure a hug he gave me at the door one Sunday morning as I was leaving the church. How easy it was for him to give me that precious memory!

Not long after I was converted, my parents took me to a revival meeting at the courthouse in Lancaster. I do not remember the preacher's name, but I recall that his family played several musical instruments and that great crowds attended the meeting. That meeting made a profound impression on me.

We attended another revival, held in a crowd-packed tobacco warehouse that had been seated for the meeting.

We attended several meetings in gospel tents after that. I listened attentively to the sermons in all those meetings. I remember none of the texts or outlines, but I do remember some of the illustrations the preachers used. From those preachers I learned the value of a good story well told. The earnestness of those revival preachers, the invitations they extended, and the people who went forward made impressions that remain with me to this day.

My First Attempt at Preaching

From the time I was saved I felt the call to preach, and I soon told some of my schoolmates that God had called me to preach. I did not own a Bible, but I found a ragged piece of a Bible that someone had discarded. I started reading and studying it, and one afternoon on the way home from school, I announced to those who were walking with me that I was going to preach them a sermon. I started preaching, and I preached by the mile instead of the clock. I ended my sermon when I turned on the drive that lead up the hill to my house. I promised to preach them another sermon the next morning. I believe I would have preached from that day, if someone had helped me get started.

God's Continuing Call

In my teen years our family stopped attending church. Not long after that I drifted and gave up the idea of preaching. I did not think of preaching again until our family returned to church, and I rededicated my life to God. By that time I did not want to preach, but every time I prayed, I knew the Lord was calling me. I made excuses, but the Lord showed me they were not reasons.

One morning about that time, Papa sent me to the back of the pasture to bring up the cows. It was a beautiful morning. The grass was wet with dew, and the morning sun was turning every dewdrop into a diamond. Morning glories were in bloom along the fence rows. The dew-wet grass came halfway to my knees, and a field-lark, startled by my tread, sprang into the sky with a plaintive cry.

That morning I had an awesome sense of the presence of God. I felt His hand upon me, and I knew He was calling me to preach. I started praying aloud as I walked. My prayer was something like this: "Lord, I don't know how to preach. I don't know how to prepare a sermon, and I don't have a voice suitable for preaching, but I believe you are calling me. If You'll give me the voice I need, and if You'll teach me what I need to know, and if You'll give me open doors and people to preach to, I'll preach for You the best I can."

I know the Lord heard that prayer. In time I learned how to prepare sermons and preach them. Doors opened to me soon after I started preaching, and people came to hear me preach. The Lord also did something for my voice. Often I have preached five or more times a day, for months at a time, and my voice has been adequate for the task. It is still serving me well.

Early Ministry

Soon after I answered the call to preach I preached my first sermon in Lancaster Baptist Church on a Wednesday night. I was almost scared to death, but I managed to get through a short message.

The following week I preached my second sermon in Mitchellsburg Baptist Church in Mitchellsburg, Kentucky. There was one convert that night, and that set my heart on fire.

Not long after that I started a revival in the Sunday school building where I had been converted. I had no sermons prepared, so I asked a preacher friend to preach every other night so I would have two days to prepare each sermon.

People in the neighborhood attended the meeting, and we had reasonably good results. My next meeting was in a schoolhouse in an adjoining county. By that time I felt that I had enough sermons to hold the meeting without another preacher helping me.

That was the beginning of the Gospel trail that has now spanned more than 75 years. In these years God has blessed me and used me far beyond anything I expected, or deserved, and I am still on the trail that will end one day beyond the gates of pearl.

Chapter 11

Travel in My Early Days

In my lifetime I have traveled in every way a person can travel except by submarine and rocket ship. Early in life I was introduced to travel on horseback, muleback, buggy, buckboard, and wagon. Later I traveled by automobile, truck, bus, and train. I also traveled by sailboats, fuel-powered boats, and airplanes. I have even ridden camelback on more than one occasion, and that is the form of riding I like least. A camel has the gait of a broken rocking chair, the breath of a waterfront bum, and the disposition of a mama grizzly bear.

Travel in a Buggy

In my early years most people depended on a horse and buggy to get around. Buggies were big business in those days. Before Papa and Mama married he worked at building buggies in

Danville, Kentucky in a factory owned and operated by his brother, Roy. One of those buggies is on display at the Kentucky Horse Park, near Lexington. It is possible that Papa worked on that buggy when he was a young man.

My grandparents owned a buggy before our family did. I remember riding with my grandmother in their buggy, pulled by a big sorrel horse named Ol' Rolly. Happily I sat by my grandmother, talking, enjoying the ride, and watching the miles go slowly by.

When the weather was cold, we wrapped ourselves in a buggy rug, and put a hot brick in the floor of the buggy to keep our feet warm. In warm weather, we sometimes encountered an unexpected rain and had to get the storm curtain from under the seat and hurriedly put it up across the front of the buggy top. The curtain kept us almost dry as we looked out at the road through a small Ison glass window.

The best trips were in warm weather. My grandmother used to hurry Ol' Rolly with the buggy whip which was mounted in a holder on the dashboard. It was my delight to use the whip to make Ol' Rolly go faster when he loitered.

Before Mama and Papa got a buggy, we rode on our mare, Liz, and our mule, Jack. Mama rode sidesaddle on the mare, and Papa rode astride the mule. I usually rode behind Papa, holding onto him. Ol' Jack was gentle, but his gait was rough. I felt as if I were going to be homogenized (though I didn't know the word) before we reached the end of a journey. Liz was a saddle mare, and it was a pleasure to ride her, though I seldom got the chance.

Finally the day came when Papa went to Danville and brought home a new Arnold Buggy he had bought from my uncle. It was black and shiny, and I thought it was beautiful. I climbed up into the seat, and Papa took me for a drive out the lane to the pike and back.

After that we enjoyed driving Liz and the buggy to Lancaster to shop and to my grandparents' home to visit. We even went to Danville in the buggy to shop and visit relatives who lived there on some occasions.

After we had had the buggy several years, Papa took the top off. I never knew why. Maybe it was just worn out. For the benefit of our young readers, when a buggy no longer had a top, it was called a buckboard—why I do not know. A buckboard looked like a dune buggy with bicycle wheels that was drawn by a horse.

We used the buckboard for several years. Mama and Papa used to ride in the seat, and I knelt in the floor in front of them with my hands on the dashboard, pretending that I was driving a car. I drove many miles that way.

Among my happiest memories were the times we drove Liz and the buckboard to church in Lancaster. We started going to church there after I was converted. Mama and I enjoyed attending church, but Papa, not a Christian at that time, soon found an excuse to stop going.

Three miles of the trip to church was on Richmond Road. It was a good, graveled road, but the increasing number of automobiles made the authorities decide to blacktop it. Country people called the blacktopped road, "The slick road." Right away Papa decided that a horse could fall and break a leg on "The slick road," so we stopped going to church. I have always thought it strange that we traveled the same slick road on Saturdays when we went to town to buy groceries, and nothing was said about the danger of the mare falling.

Our First Car

When I was eleven a salesman came to our farm from Lancaster to try to sell Papa a Model-T Ford roadster. That was a car with one seat and a cloth top. They had to work to sell cars in those days, so the car salesman drove a clean, shiny new car to our house for us to see. In those days a customer could buy a car of any color just so long as it was black.

The salesman took Mama and Papa and me a ride in the car. He gave Papa his best sales pitch, but that did not persuade him to buy the car. At last the salesman left, but he came back the next day, and again the next day. Finally he wore Papa down. Mama may have helped change his mind. At any rate, Papa decided it would be nice to own a car. He must have done some figuring during those three days—trying to decide where he would get money to pay for the car.

The price of the car was four hundred and eight dollars. That was a lot of money in those days. Papa sold a cow and half of mama's chickens and drew most of his money from the bank to come up with enough to pay cash for the car.

Papa bought the car with all the options they offered. They called them extras in those days, and they only offered two. One was called a self-starter. That meant that instead of cranking the car and taking a chance of the motor kicking backwards and breaking your arm, you could stamp on a stiff starter button in the floor, back by the seat, until you got a bruise on your heel, and the car finally started.

The other extra was called demountable rims. We had lots of flat tires in those days, and that was supposed to make it easier to fix a flat. Before demountable rims came out, tires were mounted on a rim that was part of the wheel. So you had to fix a flat tire on the roadside and take a chance on someone running over you while you were fixing it.

The demountable rim fixed all that. It was fastened to the wheel by four lug nuts, and it was relatively easy to remove. All you had to do was chock the other wheels, jack up the wheel with the flat tire, and remove the rim. A special wrench to remove the lug nuts was furnished with the car, as were the other tools that were needed to fix a flat tire.

After removing the lug nuts, you could lift the rim and tire off and carry them to the shade of a tree where you could work with tire irons for an hour to get the tire off the rim. By that time you were wet with perspiration and as dirty as if you had rolled in the dirt. There is no point in going into the details of how we used to fix flat tires. Few of my readers will ever want to try it anyway. So I'll simply say, for better or for worse, Papa bought a car with demountable rims.

The Car Liberated Us

The slick road did not bother the car. We started attending church again, and we went to places where we had never gone before. We went to camp meeting in the next county, and we went to visit my mother's sister and her family on Poosey Ridge in Madison County. Later, after they moved to Lexington, we visited them there.

While we were in Lexington, we went walking on Main Street. Mama pointed out the First National Bank building to me and told me that it was a skyscraper. I looked up at it for a long minute. Then I said: "Mama, I'd like to see it work."

Learning to Drive

I learned to drive the new Ford in mud holes. Papa wouldn't let me touch the wheel when we were on the road, but when he got the car stuck in the mud between the house and barn, he let me under the wheel so I could put the car in gear and give it gas while he pushed. With Papa pushing, the car usually came out of the mud, and I always drove it to the beginning of the graveled drive in front of the house before I stopped. I thought I could drive as well as anyone by the time I was twelve.

I had a love affair with cars, especially with Fords. Within months I was working on our car and on my grandmother's Ford touring car that she had bought the year before we bought ours. I learned to clean spark plugs and carburetors, to change distributors, to put on fan belts, to adjust the band linings in the transmission, and to adjust the spark gap in the four coils that were in a box inside the fire wall. That was about all that ever had to be done to a Model-T, short of an overhaul. Papa and I eventually learned to do that also.

To this day I remember the slow rhythm of an idling Model-T motor when both the spark and gas levers were pushed all the way up. And I remember how each coil would give a slight buzzing sound as it furnished spark to one of the spark plugs.

A Car Called a Skeeter

In those days, when a car was well-worn, boys and young men used to buy them and take the old battered, rusty body off. They bolted a wood platform on the chassis and bolted a seat to it under the steering wheel. They called this kind of vehicle a skeeter. A skeeter was much lighter than a car, so it would outrun any car on the road.

Often people who had skeeters put a cutout on them. A cutout was a gadget they bolted on the exhaust pipe, after a hole had been cut in it. A control on the floor opened and closed the cutout. When a driver opened the cutout with a skeeter running wide open, it roared like a bulldozer. It wasn't any trouble to get other traffic out of the way, especially if a Claxton horn had been put on the skeeter. The loud AH-OO-GUH sound of a Claxton horn was sufficient to drive other traffic to the ditch. Cutouts and Claxton horns were sometimes installed on regular cars as well.

My First Car

When I was about fifteen, I started wanting a car of my own, but of course there was no money to buy me a car, even if Papa had been of a mind to do so.

In those days the going price for a skeeter in running condition was around $10.00, and somehow in the next several months I managed to save money to buy one.

I drove the skeeter for a few days, but I really was not satisfied with it. I wanted a regular car. About that time someone took a body off another Ford and left it on the roadside. I asked around and found the owner. He no longer wanted the body, so he gave it to me.

I got some other boys to help, and we stripped off the floor that had been added to the skeeter. Then we managed to get the car body in place on the chassis and bolt it down. There was only one problem. The body was off of a later model car than my skeeter, so the running board brackets on the skeeter chassis were not long enough to reach the running boards on the body.

It never occurred to me to have longer brackets welded on the chassis, but I came up with my own solution. I found a 1 x 8 board long enough to reach under the car from the outer edge of one running board to the outer edge of the other one. So I jacked each running board up to level and propped it in place. Then I measured from edge to edge and cut the board the proper length. I drilled holes in the running boards and in the board and bolted the board in place. The running boards stayed level, almost, but when I stepped on the running board on the driver's side, it went down several inches, and the one on the other side went up an equal distance. It was like an upside down seesaw. I got in the car, and, when my weight came off the running board, it returned to its normal place. I took the car for a trial run. It performed perfectly, except for the running boards. They went up and down like the wings of a big bird, and each time they hit bottom, they made a loud screeching sound. I had no need for a cutout or a Claxton horn on that car. Everybody could hear me coming without them.

My Skull and Crossbones Car

My second car was a later model Ford touring car. I paid fifteen dollars for it. It was in fair mechanical condition, but some previous owner had painted a large skull and crossbones with white paint across the back of it. They had used a brush about two inches wide, so a driver following me could see that skull and crossbones almost before he saw the car. I never was comfortable driving that car, especially if some other young people went riding with me.

I soon learned why the skull and crossbones had been painted on the car. There was a mechanical curiosity about a Model-T. Underneath the car a radius rod ran between the front wheels. If by some mishap the radius rod got bent, it could be straightened, but it wouldn't stay straight, and a car with a bent radius rod behaved very strangely. It drove all right as long as the driver did not have to go around a sharp curve, but, when the steering wheel was turned beyond a certain point, the wheels would suddenly cut in the opposite direction, and the car would go out of control.

I soon discovered that the Crossbones Car had a bent radius rod, so I drove it very carefully. One day some young people went riding with me on a country road. At a sharp curve I must have forgotten about the bent radius rod and cut the wheels of the car too short. Suddenly it went out of control and ran up a steep bank. I got it stopped at the top of the bank, but the motor died, and the car rolled back down the bank. In the process it threw a tire off a front wheel, and the inner tube suddenly swelled up like a huge balloon. We all sat there and laughed as only young people can laugh. Then I had to let the air out of the tube and put the tire back on the wheel and pump it up with a hand pump. That was probably the last time I took anyone riding in that car.

Chapter 12

Travel in the Ministry

E arly in my ministry I learned that much travel is required in the Lord's work, and, with the passing of the years, the need to travel increased.

In the beginning I sometimes walked to my meetings or caught rides with others. Later I traveled in dilapidated old cars that often broke down on the road. In time I got better cars, and have traveled many thousands of miles in them

Flying Became Necessary

The need to fly arose after I held a revival in a store-front mission in Cincinnati, Ohio. Around 60 people were saved in the meeting, and the people in charge of the mission asked me to help them organize a church on a Sunday afternoon.

That was before the days of interstate highways. I was pastoring a church near Lexington, and I knew it would take four hours to drive from Lexington to Cincinnati and another four hours to return. It would not be possible for me to drive to Cincinnati, after my morning service, and return in time for my evening service. So I decided to charter a plane and fly to Cincinnati.

After we organized the church the members asked me to serve as copastor until the young preacher who had helped start the mission could gain some experience. I agreed to serve and preach for them on Sunday afternoons and Thursday nights. That made me decide to buy a plane and learn to fly. The only thing that bothered me was what I imagined would be the impossible cost of buying a plane.

One day the following week, I mentioned my thoughts about buying a plane to Harold Leggett, a Lexington engraver who frequently made halftones for me to use to print pictures in my paper. He told me he had been thinking of learning to fly and had found a used plane that was for sale for 750 dollars. We could buy the plane in partnership, and I could use it on Sundays, and he would use it during the week.

Neither of us knew anything about airplanes. If we had we would never have bought the one he had found. But, since we were blissfully ignorant, we borrowed the money and bought the plane. The plane would fly all right, and it was relatively safe. We never had a serious accident with it, but it did leave some things to be desired.

The plane was a tandem Piper Cub, Model J3. Those old Cubs, usually used as student trainers, were real workhorses, but the one we bought was not equipped the way most of them were. Every J3 Cub I have ever seen, except the one we bought, had a 65 horsepower engine. Ours had only a 50 horsepower engine, and it had single ignition. Piston powered airplanes normally have dual ignition—two magnetos, two sets of ignition wires, and two sets of spark plugs. The idea was that if one ignition failed, the other one would keep the engine running. Our plane, we learned when it was too late, had only one ignition. If it failed, the engine would stop, and we would have to make a forced landing. But we had bought the plane, and we flew it, and we never had a problem with the ignition.

The low horsepower of the engine meant that our plane had to have a longer runway than other Cubs to get off the ground. But we managed. A previous owner had installed a high speed prop on the plane, so we really had an edge in speed over the more powerful Cubs. Our plane had no radio, no running lights, no cabin lights, and no navigational instruments except a rather unreliable compass. And it had no heater, so it was icy cold in winter.

The days following the purchase of the plane were among the most exciting days of my life. I soon learned to fly and got my student permit. In a few more days I got approved for cross-country flying and started commuting between my churches every Sunday. I also started flying to revival meetings in Kentucky and surrounding states.

My partner also learned to fly, and we had many happy experiences flying together. Though I have only seen Harold Leggett once since he moved to Texas, some years ago, I have many fond memories of our association.

After I learned to fly I used to phone the airport every Sunday morning and asked them to service the plane and have it out and ready for me to fly to Cincinnati. After the morning service in my church, I drove to the airport and asked a line boy to help me get started. I transferred the lunch I had packed and my Bible to the plane. Then I went through the check list, inspecting the plane as all good pilots do. The line boy helped me untie the plane, and I got in and fastened the seat belt.

The line boy pulled the propeller to turn the engine over a time or two. Then he called, "Contact," and I turned on the ignition, and called,

"Contact," in return. He gave a quick pull on the propeller, and the engine started. I finished my checklist, ran up the engine, taxied out to the runway, took off, cleared the field, and turned north by the compass.

I ate my lunch on the way to Cincinnati. In less than an hour I crossed the Ohio River and landed at Lunkin Airport. A member of the church was there to meet me and drive me across the city to the church. After the service, I returned to the airport, refueled the plane, and took off for the flight home.

The flights each Sunday were uneventful during the summer, but with the coming of late fall, the days grew shorter, and I started running short of daylight on my return trip. I realized that in a few more weeks I would be getting back to the airport in Lexington after dark.

Preparing to Fly After Dark

The people at the airport told me that I would have to have running lights installed if I was going to fly after dark. It was not legal to fly after dark without them. Besides, it was dangerous. That was the first time I realized that other planes had running lights. My partner and I had running lights installed on the Cub. At least that would keep another plane from colliding with me in the dark.

The days grew shorter, and on Sunday afternoons after church, when I was flying home, I could see the shadows gathering in the valleys. By the time I had flown a third of the way home, I could see lights going on in houses and on storefronts, and I could see cars on the road with their headlights on.

That gave me cause for concern. The gas tank on the Cub only held 12 gallons of gasoline, enough for about three hours of flying. I knew that when the gasoline was gone, the engine would stop, and I would go down wherever I chanced to be. My only hope, I knew, was to fly straight to the airport at Lexington so I would not run out of gas.

There was always the possibility that the wind could change directions and cause the plane to drift off course. The little compass, bouncing around, was not too accurate, and it could cause me to get off course. I had no radio guidance system. At that time I did not know that one existed.

I realized it was possible that I could miss the airport and fly past it. If I did that I could run out of gas, the engine would stop, and I would crack-up and kill myself. The tension in the cockpit would start building, and I would pray and start scanning the darkening sky in the direction of the airport. I knew that if I could see the beacon light, it would guide me home.

Watching For the Beacon

After a few minutes I would see a pinpoint of green light. Then, with one hand on the throttle and the other on the control stick, I would keep my eyes on the spot where I had seen the light. Thirty seconds later I would see a flash of amber light. The drone of the engine was reassuring, and the flashing lights told me that I was on course. I would breathe a sigh of relief, relax and point the nose of the plane toward the flashing light.

Thirty minutes later I would be circling the control tower at Blue Grass Field. Because I had no radio, they had told me to box the tower—to fly rectangles around it. The man on duty in the tower would look up and say, "Here comes that crazy preacher flying his Bible" and he would turn on the runway lights.

I would circle the field, line up with the lights, and start my glide toward the runway. I would cut the throttle and the engine would slow to 1500 RPM. It was relatively quiet in the cockpit as the lights came up to meet me. Then the wheels would bump the runway, and I would thank God for the flashing lights that had guided me home.

Flying Opened Doors

Flying made me a kind of a celebrity. I was even written up by the Associated Press and some local papers because I commuted between my churches in my own plane. Perhaps I was one of the first pastors to do that. The publicity did not mean a lot to me, but I am glad I was able to reach people for the Lord by traveling in my plane.

Since that time, I have flown in many planes, even the big jets, but I have never had more fun or accomplished more good than I did while flying the J3 Cub. It enabled me to carry the Gospel to places and to people I would not otherwise have reached.

Travel in Other Ways

Much as I loved flying in my own plane, I often found it necessary to travel in other ways. While I pastored in Cincinnati, I sometimes traveled to the church on the train. I have also traveled by rail to revivals and to Bible conferences, and I have traveled by train when doing mission work in foreign lands. I have enjoyed that mode of travel since the time my grandfather took me from Hyattsville, two miles from my home, to Lancaster, a three mile ride on the train, when I was a small boy.

Travel By Sailboat

One of the most interesting journeys I ever made was by sailboat. Some of the natives in the Bahama Islands took me a day's journey, from Grand Bahama to Water Cay in a small sailboat.

There were three or more in our crew. Rev. Roy Harrison, now deceased, traveled with me. The trip to Water Cay was pleasant, but when we returned the next day, it was cold and the sea was boisterous. Brother Harrison and I spent most of the day down in the hole, hiding from the wind. It made me think of Jonah in the hole of the ship that carried him on the journey that ended with him being in a whale's belly.

God must have watched over us, for we made the trip safely, and I had the joy of preaching to the entire population of the island, except for one blind man.

Pulling a Trailer

For some years I pulled a trailer to most of my meetings that were in driving distance. It is a bit more of a hassle getting to the meetings that way, but the trailer was a great asset. It was my home away from home, and it served as an office as well. Much of my writing was done in the trailer.

In all the miles I have traveled, by every means available, God has watched over me, and I have enjoyed great success, preaching to people in many parts of America and in foreign lands.

Chapter 13

Fascination With Radio and Recorders

I have preached on radio without interruption for more than 65 years. Many have been converted through this ministry. Untold numbers have been brought closer to the Lord, and preachers and missionaries have been called into the ministry. My love of the radio ministry continues.

My First Sight of a Radio

I was a boy the first time I saw and heard a radio. One day in Lancaster, Kentucky, my mother and I heard loud music coming from the open window of an upstairs office above the First National Bank. Someone told us it was coming from a radio. We had never heard of a radio, so we decided to go up to the office and investigate. When we reached the office, we were allowed to go in and see the new contraption.

The radio covered a large table. It had a large, S shaped horn rising above it, and it had enough wires running from it to wire a small house, I thought. Tangled wires were all over the table-top. They hung over the sides of the table, and there were more wires under the table.

The looks of the contraption did not trouble us, but we were greatly puzzled that it was producing music loud enough to fill the room and spill out the window into the town below. We had no idea where the music was coming from.

Someone told us that the music was coming through the air from a distant city. That we could hardly believe. We thought it was impossible for music to come through the air.

We talked about the radio all the way home and for many days after that. Finally we learned that the radio really had been invented, and that by some miracle we did not understand, it could catch sounds that were produced many miles away. We decided that someday we would have a radio.

Our First Radio

After I had become a teenager we bought a used radio. It was in a small wood case, designed to set on a tabletop. It had only two vacuum tubes, and it was battery powered. Instead of a speaker, then called a horn, it had two sets of headphones. Only two people could listen to it at a time, but oh how we enjoyed that radio. Sometimes we took one of the phones off the head bracket so Papa, Mama and I could all listen at the same time.

I soon learned that a long, high antenna and a good ground would enable the radio to bring in distant stations. So I strung antenna wire between the top of our house and the top of the barn, a hundred yards away. After that it was great fun to tune in stations from distant cities at night. (We could not get them in the daytime.) We kept a list of the distant stations, and tried to get them again. The same stations did not come in every night.

Often we were up late at night listening to the radio, and I turned it on as soon as I got out of bed the next morning. All the stations had live performers in those days, and I found a powerful station in Del Rio, Texas, that had a young musician on at 4:00 a.m. that I really liked. After that I missed very few mornings tuning in that station to hear him play the guitar and sing.

A Better Radio

In time we got a better radio, complete with A batteries, B batteries, and a C battery. It also had a loud speaker. With great excitement, I figured out how to hook the radio to the batteries and to the antenna and ground wires. Then we turned it on and thrilled at all the things that came out of the speaker.

We soon found some special programs that we listened to every day. At night we listened to Lowell Thomas and the news, and we listened to Kate Smith sing, *God Bless America* and other good songs. I doubt that Lowell Thomas has ever been equaled as a newscaster. He told it like it was without telling us what we were supposed to think about it. And few singers have entertained a generation of Americans as Kate Smith did.

Hearing Preaching on Radio

We soon found *The Nation's Family Prayer Period* on WLW in Cincinnati. It was broadcast from Cadle Tabernacle in Indianapolis early each weekday morning and at noon on Sundays. E. Howard Cadle was pastor of the tabernacle and speaker on the broadcast.

Mrs. Cadle warmed our hearts each morning by singing the theme, *Ere you left your room this morning, did you think to pray?* After another song, Buford Cadle presented his father, and he preached a homespun sermon with compassion and power. Few, if any, radio broadcasters preached the gospel to as many at that time as Mr. Cadle did on *The Nation's Family Prayer*

Period.

After Dr. B. R. Lakin became copastor of the tabernacle we listened to him on the days when he did the broadcast. Little did I dream then that one day Dr. Lakin and I would become friends and that I would follow him on a radio network program he had founded.

After I answered the call to preach, I knew right away that I wanted to preach on radio. My first radio broadcast was over a small, home-built, bootleg radio station that was on the air for two or three hours each Sunday morning. Much later, after I became pastor of a church in East Kentucky, I drove more than a hundred miles to speak on a program that was conducted by a preacher I knew.

My First Radio Ministry

I started my first regular broadcast on a station in Williamson, West Virginia. After I moved to Ashland, Kentucky, I went on radio there for a time. In 1942, after I moved to Lexington, I started broadcasting on a Lexington station. I have been on without interruption since then. I believe my broadcast is the longest running religious broadcast in the nation.

The Voice of the Appalachians

Dr. B. R. Lakin started *The Voice of the Ap-*

palachians Network, after he left Cadle Tabernacle. In his later years, because of failing health, he gave the program to me. I preached on *The Voice* for 21 years, then turned it over to Dr. Jeff Fugate. He continues to preach on The *Voice* on a number of stations every week

While I was preaching on *The Voice* I learned that many of the people who had heard Dr. Lakin and Mr. Cadle preach were still listening to the program. After I turned *The Voice* over to Dr. Fugate, I continued to preach on my program, *Preaching at Your House.* As this is being written, I am still conducting that program daily except on Saturdays.

My Interest in Recorders

From the time I was a teenager, I was interested in recording machines. I have watched them evolve from crude mechanical devices to the sophisticated recorders we have today. Recorders of one sort or another have long been a vital part of radio broadcasting, and I have used many of them.

The following is a bit of the history of the evolution of the recorders we use today.

In 1877, Thomas A. Edison invented the first sound recorder. It was a primitive contraption with a cylinder made of wax and tinfoil. To test the machine, Edison had one of his assistants turn the cylinder with a crank while he shouted into a horn, the nursery rhyme, *Mary Had a Little Lamb.* At the small end of the horn was a diaphragm with a needle attached to it. The needle cut a vibrating track in the cylinder. The sound played back when the needle was again made to run in the track.

In time Edison came out with a phonograph with recordings made on cylinders. A large morning-glory shaped horn amplified the sound mechanically. A later model of Edison's phonograph had a turntable that played a recording from a thick disk. Several other companies soon produced phonographs, similar in design but not compatible with the Edison machine. The phonograph has been called by many names, such as, the gramophone, the victrola, the record player, and the stereo.

The first major improvement in these machines was the introduction of electronically recorded sound. The sound was further enhanced when played back on an electronic record player.

For a number of years recordings were pressed on shellac disk that played back at 78 RPM. The shellac recordings were eventually replaced by vinyl disk that were less scratchy, and had better sound quality. Not long after that, the industry came out with 45 RPM singles and 33 and 1/3 RPM long-play albums. Stereo sound soon followed. Now we have even better sound from digitally recorded devices, but I have never enjoyed any records as much as I did the ones we played on the victrola Mama ordered from a Sears and Roebuck catalog when I was a boy. Some of our neighbors had better victrolas long before we got ours, but they could not have enjoyed them any more than we did ours. Often I had gone to listen to their records on their victrola, but it was different after we got our own victrola and could invite them to come to our house to hear our records.

Recording For Radio

Early in my radio ministry I found it necessary to record some of my broadcasts. In the beginning I used recorders that cut grooves in acetate disks and recorded sound on them in one pass. They were far from satisfactory, so other means of recording were invented. As far as I know, the earliest of these was the wire recorder. It was soon replaced by tape recorders. Next came the cassette tape recorder, and soon many Americans were carrying small cassette recorders around with them and making their own recordings.

The early tape recordings used 1/4 inch, reel to reel to reel tapes. They were bulky and heavy, and the quality of recordings made on them was not good. Later models did make good recordings, and they became the standard for radio broadcasting for a time.

When the cassette recorder came along, with its smaller tape and slower speed, it was not considered good enough to use for serious broadcasting. But soon the dolby enhancement and other refinements improved the quality, and most radio stations started using them.

Then record companies started putting music on cassettes. Digital recording improved cassettes still more, but they were soon replaced by exceptionably good quality CDs. Now much recording is done on computers.

I used to record radio broadcasts far into the night before leaving for a meeting. I now have it a bit more organized, but I still have to make recordings ahead when I am going to be away for an extended time.

Recording is Not New

Man's ability to record both sound and pictures brings to mind the fact that God was recording long before man ever thought of doing it. There are several verses in the Bible that tell us of God making a record of all that we say and do. There is a most interesting verse in Psalm 87:6, *The LORD shall count, when he writeth* up the people, that this man was born there. Selah." This indicates that God makes a record of each person's life, including his birthplace.

In Matthew 10:30 and Luke 12:7 we are told that the hairs of our heads are numbered, and in Ecclesiastes 12:14 we are told that God will bring every secret thing to judgment. In Revelation 20 we are told that the books will be opened at the judgment of the wicked dead. So it appears that God has some good methods of recording and keeping records. This should challenge us to walk circumspectly before our God.

Chapter 14

Car Travel Miracles

If I had no Bible, and if I had never heard of God, I would still believe in His existence. I have seen Him do too many wonderful things to ever doubt that He lives and that He is a loving, all-powerful God.

In my years of walking with God, I have seen some big miracles and more than my share of small miracles. I trust that the sharing of some of them will strengthen the faith of those who read about them. Because of the many miles I have traveled in the ministry, many of the miracles I have seen have been travel miracles.

Gas on a Winter Night

One winter night when the temperature was 15 below zero, I was returning from the church I pastored in Belfry, Kentucky to my home in Warfield. Most of the trip was through West Virginia. About midnight my motor started missing, and I realized that I had forgotten to buy gasoline.

I let the car coast to the side of the road and stop. I looked around and saw that I had stopped in front of a country gas station. Someone lived upstairs over the station, and the light was on. Believing that my problem was solved, I climbed the steps and knocked on the door.

"Who is it?" a man answered.

"I'm a Baptist preacher, and I'm out of gas," I returned.

"That's your problem. I'm closed, and I'm not going to come down and open the station for you," the man answered.

I begged and pleaded, but to no avail. I told the man I would freeze before daylight if I did not get some gas, but he refused to come out and open the station.

Finally I walked back down the stairs, stopped behind my car, closed my eyes and prayed that God would send me some gas.

When I opened my eyes I saw a tiny crack of light that appeared to be coming from a building a hundred yards or more away. I moved my head slightly, and I could no longer see the light. I moved my head back and saw the crack of light. I moved my head in the other direction and the light disappeared. If I had not been standing in the exact spot where I stopped to pray I would not have seen the light.

I started walking toward the light, being careful not to loose sight of it. After climbing a fence and crossing several railroad tracks I came to a boxcar and heard some men talking inside.

I rapped on the side of the boxcar and someone asked who I was. I told him I was a preacher and that I was out of gasoline.

"That's no problem. We have a 50 gallon drum full of gas in the next boxcar," he answered.

He came out, led the way to the next boxcar, and filled a 5 gallon can with gas. Then he walked with me to my car and poured the gas in the tank. He would not take any pay for the gas, so I thanked him and continued on my way, realizing that God had performed a miracle

Gas in the Rain

Some years later, I was driving home from a broadcast on a radio station in Winchester, Kentucky, about eighteen miles from where I lived. On the way I was caught in an unusually hard rainstorm. About that time my motor sputtered, and I realized that I had forgotten to fill the gas tank.

I guided the car out of the road and it stopped on a grassy shoulder. Then I looked out the window at the pouring rain and started praying. I told the Lord it was my fault that I had run out of gasoline, and I was sorry. I also told Him that I didn't mind walking after gas, but it was raining, and I would get wet on the way to a gas station. I would likely get a cold, and that would make me sound terrible on the radio. I then asked the Lord to either stop the rain or send me some gasoline.

A moment later a pickup truck stopped beside my car. The man in the truck rolled down his window, and I rolled down my window.

"Why, Preacher, I almost didn't recognize your car in all this rain," he said. "What's your trouble?"

"I'm out of gas," I replied, wondering who he was and how he had recognized my car. I did not remember having seen him before.

"I just happen to have some gas in a can in the back of my truck. Don't get out and get wet. I'm wearing a raincoat, and I'll put the gas in your car."

He parked in front of me, got a five gallon can of gas from the back of his pickup truck, and poured it in my gas tank.

"What do I owe you?" I asked as he came to my window.

"Not a thing. The Lord sent that gas to you. This morning as I started to leave home, I had a sudden impression that I ought to go back to the garage and get the five gallon can of gas I had there and put it in the truck. I had no idea why, but now I know. The Lord knew you were going to run of gas, so He told me to put that can of gas in my truck." I was amazed. In Isaiah 65:24 God promised to answer prayers during the millennial before people prayed. The millennial had not come, but God had answered my prayer before I prayed. I thanked the Lord for the answer and continued on my way.

Oil on a Mountain

Some years ago, one of the men of the church I was pastoring went with me to Florida in my pickup truck. On our way home a few days later, the motor started missing badly. I stopped at a garage, and a mechanic told me that the motor appeared to have a cracked piston. He thought I could drive home before getting it repaired, though it would probably use a lot of oil.

My friend and I wanted to get home, so we decided to drive the truck as it was. The mechanic was right about it using oil. We had to add oil every few miles. I finally bought a case of oil, thinking that would be enough to take us the rest of the way home. But the condition of the motor worsened, and it started using even more oil.

Before starting up Jellico Mountain in Tennessee, I poured the last quart of oil I had in the motor. Before we reached the top of the mountain, the oil pressure dropped, and I pulled the truck to the side of the road and stopped. We were miles from a gas station.

"What do we do now?" my friend asked.

"First we pray," I replied. I bowed my head and asked the Lord to send us some oil.

Minutes later a run-down old jalopy of a car stopped. "Are you broke down?" a man asked.

"I'm low on oil," I told him. "My truck is throwing oil out."

"My car wastes oil too, so I carry a case with me all the time," he said. He got two quarts of oil from the trunk of his car and brought them to me. "This ought to last 'til you get to a gas station in Jellico," he said. "It's downhill most the way from here."

He refused to let me pay for the oil, so I thanked him and watched him drive on. We thanked the Lord, poured the oil in the crankcase of the truck, and started on. In Jellico we bought enough oil to last the rest of the way home.

Jumper Cables in a Hurry

One day I was running late on my way to a revival in Ohio. About a hundred miles from the church where I was to hold the meeting, I pulled into a rest area and turned off the ignition. I went in, and when I returned a few minutes later, the battery was down, and the motor would not start. I told the Lord that I was running late and asked Him to send help. Then I raised the hood of my car and stood by it waiting.

In a few minutes a car, pulling a U-haul trailer, came into the rest area on the other side of the median. The driver parked, got out, and looked my way. Then he got back in his car, did a U-turn in the parking area, drove the wrong way to the end of the median, then turned and drove to where I was parked.

"What's your trouble?" he called as he stopped.

"My battery is down."

"I have some jumper cables, and I'll start your car," he said.

He started my car, drove out of the rest area and hurried on his way, as if he had only stopped to help me. I thanked the Lord, continued on to my meeting, and arrived on time

Preservation on Snow-covered Knob

When one drives the highways as much as I do, there are sometimes close calls. The way I was delivered from some of them makes them qualify as miracles. One of the close calls occurred one night long ago, when I was driving home after preaching in a church in the Knob section in Boyle County, Kentucky.

It started snowing before I reached the church, and by the time the service was over, there was an inch or more of snow on the ground. I did not mind driving in the snow, but I was concerned about getting over the steep knob on the narrow, snow-covered, country road.

The car did considerable skidding on the way up the knob, but I reached the top without mishap. The road was much steeper going down the other side, so I put the car in low gear, thinking that would cause it to go down the hill slowly, but that did not work. Instead the car started skidding like a runaway sleigh. I had to fight the steering wheel to keep the skidding car on the narrow road, and there was nothing I could do to slow its speed.

The last hundred yards of the road was almost straight down, and it made a sharp turn at the bottom of the hill. When the car reached the steep place it gained speed, and I was sure I could not make the curve at the bottom of the hill. Only a miracle would keep the car from crashing into a ravine, and that could mean injury or death.

I prayed as the car approached the curve, and it suddenly slowed, went around the curve without the slightest skid, and stopped. It felt as if a giant hand had controlled the car. I thanked the Lord and started on.

Ice on Mountain Highway

Another life-saving miracle occurred in the

mountains of East Kentucky. This miracle took place one day when I was traveling from Inez, Kentucky, where I was pastoring, to visit my parents in my boyhood home near Lancaster, Kentucky. It was a winter day, and the two-lane road was covered with snow and ice.

In those days the highway department did not clean the snow off the roads as they do today, and there were no guardrails on the sides of roads. If a car went out of control in some places, it could plunge hundreds of feet to the valley below.

When I reached the top of a large mountain and started down the other side, my car skidded out of control and started spinning down the mountain. There was nothing I could do but pray. In a moment the car stopped spinning and headed toward the side of the road. There was no way I could keep it from going over the side and crashing into the valley

Then a miracle occurred. The car stopped with the front wheels hanging over the edge of the precipice. God must have sent an angel to stop the car. To my surprise I was able to back the car into the road and continue on my way.

Miracle on a Bridge

Years ago I preached on a snowy Sunday morning at Liberty Baptist Church in Buckeye, Kentucky, the village where I was born and where I was then pastoring. That afternoon I started driving the nine miles to Lancaster. The road was coated with ice, so I had to drive cautiously.

I soon started down a small hill toward a one-lane bridge. There was a curve just beyond the bridge. As I was approaching the bridge a car came around the curve, picking up speed to get up the hill. When the driver saw my car he applied brakes, and his car started skidding. There was no way he could stop before he reached the bridge.

I tried to stop my car, and it also started skidding. Both cars entered the bridge at the same time, and it appeared that they were going crash, head-on. That was another time I prayed.

I braced for the crash, but a miracle occurred. When the cars were about to crash, the front end of each car started skidding to their right. Then it appeared that the sides of the cars were going to collide, but at that instant both cars started skidding to their left. They passed without touching. My car barely missed the abutment of the bridge on my left, and the other car barely missed the abutment on its left. Neither car received a scratch.

I could hardly believe what had happened. I thought that the bridge must have been wider than I thought, so I stopped my car and went back and measured it. Sure enough, it was too narrow for two cars to pass. I had been saved by a miracle.

That was a small miracle for God to perform, but it was a big miracle to me. It saved my car, and it may have kept me and the other driver from being injured.

My Car Protected

For years it was my practice to drive home at night after closing a meetings. In the winter months I often had to travel in bad weather.

One night when I was driving home on a snow-covered road from a meeting in northern Ohio, God kept my car from being damaged. I drove cautiously and reached Cincinnati without difficulty, but when I started across the Ohio River bridge to Kentucky it was coated with ice. When I was near the Kentucky side of the bridge, a car coming toward me went out of control, and started spinning. I stopped my car and waited for the crash, but, just before the car reached me it stopped spinning, turned to my left, and ran into the side of the bridge. My car was unharmed. It is possible that God sent an angel to protect it.

My Car Spared Again

Years ago, when I was pastoring in Louisville, Kentucky, Mrs. Arnold and I were making some visits one Sunday afternoon. It was a beautiful day, the streets were dry, and we did not think of the possibility of being involved in an accident.

I stopped our car at the end of a street and waited for the traffic to clear so I could make a turn to the left. Then a car, approaching from the right, started turning toward our car. I pressed hard on my brake pedal and waited for a crash that I could not avoid, but, at the last instant a strange thing occurred. A car coming from my left clipped the bumper of the car that was about to hit our car. That turned the car enough to make it miss our car. It went across the street, and hit an electric pole. No one was hurt, our car was spared, and we were able to continue making visits. God had protected our car in a strange way.

Protection in an Accident

On June 11, 1998, I was involved in an accident that totaled the van I was driving. At one o'clock in the morning, I was seven miles from home from a meeting in West Virginia when the driver of a one and a half ton truck ran a stoplight and hit my van on the driver's side. The front door was demolished, and the van was knocked off the road and into a guardrail. It bounced off the guardrail, switched ends, turned over on the passenger side, skidded on the highway, and came back up on its wheels.

The van was a total wreck. The center of the steering wheel came out, rearview mirror came off and was thrown into the back seat, and the spare tire cover was thrown into the field beyond the guardrail.

My glasses were torn from my face and landed on the highway. The pen that was clipped in my shirt pocket was also thrown out on the highway, and I would have been thrown out on the highway if I had not been wearing a seat belt.

It is a miracle that I was not killed. One of the ambulance drivers, who raced to the scene, asked me over and over if I was all right. One of the officers at the scene asked me the same question, then proceeded to check my coordination. Finally he said, "Someone was looking after you. I wondered if you were still out there preaching." A witness to the accident said, "Someone was looking out for him."

My life was spared, and I suffered no injury. I only had one mildly sore place where I hit the arm rest and a small scratch on by back. I was fine the next day and put in a full day in my office. I did a usual day's work, including my broadcast.

They took the driver of the truck to the hospital, then to jail for driving under the influence of alcohol. After he got out I had the joy of leading him to the Lord. He went to church with his wife the following Sunday.

Chapter 15

Summary of My Ministry

While I was struggling with the call to preach—feeling that I was called, yet not willing to surrender, my English teacher, Miss Conrad, asked me to enter the high school oratorical contest. I was too timid to enter the contest, but I was never good at saying no, so I let her talk me into it. Of all things, she gave me a sermon by D. L. Moody to memorize and recite in the contest. Dutifully I memorized the sermon, and she coached me on how to stand and how to speak.

The night of the contest most of the students and many of the townspeople were there. I was a freshman competing against seniors, but I did my best. Later they told me the judges wanted to award me first place, but they were reluctant to choose a freshman over a senior. That did a lot for my ego.

My Early Ministry

After I answered the call to preach, my pastor, Roy Gabbard, asked me to preach my first sermon at prayer meeting on a Wednesday night. The next week I went with him to a revival he was holding in the Baptist Church at Mitchellsburg, Kentucky. The second night I went with him again, and he asked me to preach. So I started preaching almost from the day I answered the call.

That summer I engaged in revival work. I preached and led singing in meetings through most of the summer, and I had good crowds and good results. I had no meetings after the first of September, but through the fall and winter, I studied my Bible, read books by Moody and others and prayed for the Lord to open doors for me.

My First Pastorate

Without my knowing it, the Lord was already working on my behalf. The night my pastor asked me to preach at Mitchellsburg, the Lord gave us a good service, and the people did not forget me. Several months later, after their pastor had resigned, they talked among themselves about me and wondered how to get in touch with me.

About that time one of the ladies from the church visited a home about twenty miles from Mitchellsburg. While she was there she mentioned that her church was looking for a pastor, and they told her that a young preacher sometimes visited next door.

"Tell him to contact us," the visitor said, though she had no idea I was the young preacher the people at Mitchellsburg wanted to locate. It was a miracle how God worked that all out.

Before long I was told of the conversation, and I decided to help the people of the church find me. I drove to Mitchellsburg and asked how to get in touch with one of the church leaders.

I was told that Howard Preston was one of the deacons, and that he was working on the road on the other side of the knob from Mitchellsburg.

I drove my car up the knob, but when I started down the other side, the road was muddy and torn up. So I parked and started walking. Halfway down the knob, I saw a man walking toward me, laughing.

"Where in the world did you come from?" he called when I was in hearing distance.

"I heard you people are looking for a pastor," I called back.

"We are."

We met and shook hands.

"When can you preach for us?" he asked.

"Next Sunday," I answered.

"I'll announce that you're coming, and we'll be expecting you," he replied.

I preached in the Mitchellsburg Baptist Church the next Sunday, and they called me to be their pastor. A week later, I preached in Salem Baptist Church, located about two miles from where I had met Howard Preston on the knob. They also called me. I accepted the call to serve both churches half time, and I was in the ministry full time. I have been in the ministry full time ever since. I came to know and love the people of both churches, and many fond memories of those days remain with me.

At that time Mitchellsburg, a crossroads village, boasted a railroad station, a post office, two stores, three churches and perhaps twenty-five or thirty houses.

The attendance at Mitchellsburg was not more than 35 when I became pastor there. The attendance at Salem was even smaller, but I could not have been more excited if both churches had had a thousand in attendance.

God's Blessings at Mitchellsburg

The attendance Mitchellsburg did not long remain at 35. By the time I held my own revival that summer, both the building and the yard were filled with people. Many were converted, and the church grew rapidly.

The people were patient with a young, inexperienced pastor, but some of them were not above putting me in my place when they thought I had stepped out of bounds.

The Work at Salem

Salem Baptist Church was on Scrub Grass Creek, three miles over the knob from where I had moved in Mitchellsburg. In the winter, when my car would not start, I walked the three miles and crossed the creek four or five times. I had to place stepping-stones in the creek at each crossing and step carefully on them as I crossed.

On such Sundays the attendance was small, and we huddled around a potbellied heating stove, and sang and prayed, and studied God's Word. After Sunday school, I preached to them. During the good weather, in the spring, summer, and fall, the attendance was good for a country church. Often the church was filled, and God gave us some blessed services.

The people at Salem loved me, fed me on Sundays, challenged me often, and sometimes tried me. I remember an elderly lady shaking hands with me at the door one Sunday morning and saying, "That was a nice little talk. If you keep on trying, someday you'll make a preacher." That really punctured my balloon. Here I was, a young D. L. Moody, and she had just called my great sermon, "a little talk."

I had a lot to learn when I started pastoring at

Mitchellsburg and Salem, but the people put up with my blunders, encouraged me, and prayed for me. I became a better preacher because of them.

A Miracle of Foresight

While I was pastoring at Mitchellsburg and Salem I attended a Bible school at Russell, Kentucky. One day when classes were over for the week I felt led to catch a bus and go to Lexington. I could think of no reason why I should go, but the impression was so strong it was as if the Lord had spoken to me.

I prayed and told the Lord that I had no reason to go to Lexington. Besides, I did not have money for bus fare. Then I told the Lord that if He really wanted me to go, He would have to pay my way.

Minutes later another student approached me and said that God had told him to give me some money. He gave me just enough to pay my fare to Lexington. I thanked him, and a short time later I boarded the bus.

It was almost dark when the bus arrived in Lexington. I got off, walked outside the station and asked the Lord where I was supposed to go. Instantly, I was reminded that I had a cousin who lived in Lexington. I had not seen him in a long time, and I felt impressed to go to his house.

At that time city bus fare was only five cents to anywhere in the city, but I did not have five cents. So I walked to where my cousin lived.

When I arrived I found him seated by a fire in a grate. He greeted me warmly and asked if I had had supper. I told him that I had not. He had not had supper either, so he cooked bacon and eggs in a skillet over the open fire. When it was ready we ate together before the fire. When we finished eating, he put the dishes away and we sat before the fire and talked.

"Are you still preaching?" he asked after a while.

"Yes, God called me to preach, and I will preach as long as I live. Are you still unsaved?"

"I really don't know how to be saved," he said. "I know Jesus died on the cross, but I don't know what that has to do with being saved."

I then told him why Jesus came to the world, and why He died on the cross. I gave him the Gospel the best I could. He asked many questions, and I did my best to answer them. We sat before the fire talking for hours, but I could not get him to receive Jesus as his Saviour.

"I never knew until now that Jesus died for my sins," he finally said.

The following summer I became ill with typhoid fever and was confined to my bed for about six weeks. During my illness my cousin was mortally wounded in a fight. I could not visit him in the hospital, but before he died he sent word to me that he had trusted Jesus as his Saviour. Not until then did I understand why God had led me to ride the bus to Lexington and spend the night with my cousin. That was a miracle of the leading of the Lord.

Coal in a Blizzard

I pastored at Mitchellsburg and Salem toward the end of the great depression. Money was in short supply, and my salary form both churches was about 35 dollars a month. From that small salary I had to pay rent and a small monthly payment on my car. So, when winter came, instead of buying fuel, I cut down small trees in a nearby forest, drug them to the lot beside the house by hand and cut them into firewood.

That was all right in mild weather, but a winter blizzard came, and it was so cold the heating stove burned wood faster than I could cut it. I spent the first day of the blizzard cutting wood, and that night we burned almost all I had cut. We needed coal, but we did not have a phone, and I could not order coal from the coal yard 10 miles away. Besides, the roads were covered with ice, and little traffic was moving. Most everyone was needing coal, and, even if I had a way to order coal, there was little chance that it could be delivered that day.

In spite of the bad roads, about midmorning a small truck, loaded with coal, stopped in front of our house, and a man I did not know knocked on my door and asked if I wanted to buy some coal. He could have stopped in front of any house along the way but he continued ten miles to the house where I lived. God sent him to my door with the coal I needed.

Food Sent Over Icy Roads

During the blizzard, we also needed food. The morning after the blizzard started we ate the last food we had for breakfast. There was a small grocery store in Mitchellsburg, but it was five miles away, and I could not get my car out of the driveway.

The food that was delivered to our house may not qualify as a miracle because my parents brought it. The miracle was that my mother sensed that we needed food, and that my father, never a good driver, was able to negotiate twenty-five miles of icy roads from their house to our house to bring the food. At any rate they arrived before noon with their car loaded with groceries. We never missed a meal.

Power for the Task

I remember a talk I had with the Lord one day as I climbed the knob on foot, on my way from Salem to Mitchellsburg. I asked the Lord to give me the power He had given D. L. Moody, and it seemed that the Lord said, "Son, when you get Moody's crowd, I'll give you Moody's power. For the present, I'll give you all the power you need to pastor Mitchellsburg and Salem Baptist Churches."

After I left the pastorates at Mitchellsburg and Salem, I pastored Liberty Baptist Church in Garrard County for a year. Then I pastored Wallaceton Baptist Church in Madison County for a year. After that I went to the First Baptist Church at Inez, in the mountains of East Kentucky.

While I was in East Kentucky, I organized the Warfield Baptist Church from a meeting I held in an abandoned church building. More than 80 people were baptized after the meeting and became charter members of the church.

The First Baptist Church at Inez was a mission church. The Kentucky Baptist State Mission Board supplemented the small salary the church paid, but my income was still far from adequate.

My First Desk

When I moved in the parsonage at Inez, I reserved one small room for an office. I had a used portable typewriter I had bought for $10.00, but I did not have a desk. I had to make do with an old kitchen table. I longed for a desk, but I did not have money to buy one, nor did I have money to buy the lumber to build one.

After I had been at Inez about a year, one of my members started building a house next door to the parsonage. Each day the carpenters threw out scraps of lumber, and I started wondering if there would be any scraps large enough for me to use to build a desk. To my despair they threw out nothing that was large enough.

Then one day, about the time they were finishing the house, some workmen delivered a new refrigerator in a wooden shipping crate. My new neighbor removed the crate and threw it out with the scrap lumber. The minute I saw the crate, I started wondering if I could make a desk of it. I turned it on its side and saw that it was made of very thin plywood, reinforced at the corners by one inch strips of rough lumber.

I reasoned that the crate had been strong enough to protect the refrigerator while it was being shipped across the country. Surely it would be strong enough to make a desk. I would only have to cut it to the needed size, cut out a place in the front for my knees, cut openings for drawers, and make a strong top for it.

More excited than I wanted my neighbor to realize, I asked him if I could have the crate and some of the scrap lumber to use to make a desk.

Looking devious, he said I could take what I needed. So I carried the crate home and started working on it.

I had no power tools, and the few hand tools I had were old and dull, so it was hard work and it was slow. I cut the crate to the size of a small desk, cut an opening for my knees and openings for the drawers—two on each side and one above the knee opening. I built the drawers from some of the larger scraps of lumber. Then I went to the grocery store and asked for some empty wood apple crates. From these I made drawer fronts.

I found some short pieces of pine flooring and used them to make the top of the desk. I used pieces of molding to reinforce the corners and to cover the rough edges of the top.

It must have taken me a day or two to hand sand all the rough places off the desk. Then I stained it with cherry oil stain. The stain was much redder than cherry. It really was bright after I varnished it, but I still thought it was a beautiful desk, and my only expense for it had been the cost of a few finish nails, some sandpaper, some putty, some oil stain, some varnish, and some inexpensive plastic drawer pulls.

I moved it to the room I was using for an office, then put paper, envelopes, pencils, and paper clips in the drawers. I placed the portable typewriter on top of the desk, brought a chair from the kitchen, and I was in business.

No preacher could ever have been more pleased with a desk than I was with mine. I used that desk when I was preparing sermons, answering mail, and keeping records. I even wrote the first draft of my first novel and the beginning of several others on that desk. When I moved to my next church, I moved that desk with me. Through the years, I have continued to move it everywhere I have gone.

While I was pastor in Ashland, Kentucky, a few years later, I bought a chair to match the desk, and I thought I really was getting up in the world. I have a picture of me, sitting at the desk, looking very pastoral, after I moved from Ashland to Central Kentucky. I am still using that desk in my broadcast studio.

I am not sure when I finally got prosperous enough to buy a regular desk, but the day did come. A few years ago, I bought the large desk I am now using. It is great for the work I do, but it will never invoke the memories that my first desk does.

God Stopped the Rain

I went from the pastorate at Inez to a church I had organized at Warfield. While I was there a brother preacher and I started a broadcast on a radio station in Williamson, West Virginia. The program soon generated so much interest, we started holding open-air services on Pond Creek, across the Kentucky line from Williamson. Good crowds attended from the beginning, and people were converted in the services. These street meetings soon led to the organization of the Belfry Baptist Church.

For the outdoor services we set up a pulpit in an open area, not far off the highway. We hooked up a loudspeaker, and passed out hymnbooks to the people as they gathered for the service. I do not recall whether we had a musical instrument or not.

One afternoon just as we started the service, there was a rumble of thunder and a rush of wind. Dark clouds swept across the sky. Big raindrops started splattering on the pavement and wetting the people, and there was a sudden rush as they started to leave.

I stepped to the microphone and said in a loud voice, "Just a minute. We are going to ask God to stop the rain until the service is over."

Most of the people stopped where they were while I prayed. At once the wind abated, and the clouds started moving away from us. We continued with the service and had good results.

After the service, as we were taking down our equipment, a man drove up in a thoroughly drenched automobile. "Didn't it rain here?" he asked, looking puzzled.

"We asked God to stop the rain, and He did," I told him.

"It washed everything away a half mile down the road," he declared, shaking his head in dismay. About that time someone came from the other direction and told us that there had been a flood of rain a half mile up the road.

In the press of passing years, I had forgotten this event. Then on the day when I was observing my fiftieth anniversary in the ministry, a man stood up during the opening exercise and told that he had been present the day God stopped the rain.

Besides pastoring at Warfield, I pastored in Johnson and Pike counties before going to Central Baptist Church in Ashland, Kentucky. From Central Baptist, I moved to the South Elkhorn Baptist Church in Fayette County.

Organizing Rosemont Baptist Church

After resigning at South Elkhorn I held a tent revival on the south side of Lexington. At the end of the two-week meeting I organized the Rosemont Baptist Church with 70 charter members. The church was full time from its beginning, and I had the privilege of being their first pastor.

Organizing Fellowship Baptist Church

I left Rosemont to go into evangelism for a

time. Then, in 1950 I organized the Fellowship Baptist Church on the north side of Lexington. There were 70 charter members and others awaiting baptism when the church was organized. For a time Fellowship Baptist worshiped in a rented building. After the building burned, the church bought property and built an auditorium that 2000 people could crowd into.

The day we dedicated Fellowship Baptist Church, an estimated four thousand people tried to attend the service. Cars filled the parking lot and every available space on nearby streets and blocked all roads leading to the church. Half the people never got in to attend the service.

Fellowship Baptist Church grew rapidly, and soon people were coming to services every Sunday from every adjoining county. They overworked the men in charge of parking and kept several ushers busy seating them. People were constantly being saved and uniting with the church. In one period of 18 months, we did not miss a single service, including Wednesday night prayer meetings, having people saved. Often on Sunday mornings 10 to 25 people came forward at the close of the service to receive the Lord as Saviour.

At that time my daily radio broadcasts blanketed Central Kentucky daily from three stations. That was before TV came to the region, and there were not many radio stations to divide the audience. Almost everybody listened to our program. That was a contributing factor to the rapid growth of the church.

The Power of Radio

The following is an example of the power of radio in those days. In January, 1948, I scheduled a Sunday afternoon service in the courthouse at Danville, Kentucky. I announced the service on my daily radio program and on the Sunday program. I may have placed a small ad in the Danville paper.

On the Saturday night before the planned service, a blizzard struck Central Kentucky and brought freezing rain and sleet. By Sunday morning all roads were ice-coated and almost impassible. I doubted that very few would venture out for the service in Danville in such weather and on such hazardous roads, but I did not want to disappoint any who did come.

After the morning service in my church and a hurried lunch we started driving to Danville on the ice-coated roads. The roads were so bad it was past time for the service to start when we reached the courthouse. To my amazement, I saw people lined up for a city block trying to get in the building. I thought perhaps the door was locked, but when I reached the door, I found that it was blocked with people, and the stairway leading up to the courtroom on the second floor was packed with people standing four abreast on each stair tread. I was told that the courtroom was also packed with people.

I had to go to the rear of the building and go up a back stairway to reach the crowded courtroom. When I entered, a deacon from the First Baptist Church stood up and got my attention.

"There is no way this crowd can get in here, and it's too cold for people to stand outside," he said. "The First Baptist Church is directly behind the courthouse. I'll go open the door and you can have the service there. Tell the people on the stairs to turn around and go down so the people in here can get out, and they can all march around the block to the church."

I made the announcement, and the people at the head of the stairs relayed the word to the ones below them. They passed the word along to the people outside the door, and they passed the word to those who were lined up along the block. Those at the end of the line started walking toward the church, and the others followed. I doubt that I lost anyone in the move. Soon the large auditorium and balcony of the First Baptist Church were filled with people, and there were many standing after all the seats were taken.

The service started late, but no one seemed to

mind. I had great liberty preaching, and the presence of the Lord was very real in the service. More than 25 adults came forward to receive Christ as Saviour at the close of the service. My radio ministry brought that great crowd together in spite of the ice storm.

Blessings Through the Years

I have had the joy of organizing several churches and seeing other churches grow out of my ministry. I pastored some of these churches. Among them was one in Warfield, one in Belfry, two in Cincinnati, one in Louisville, four in Lexington, and one in Campbellsville.

In the 1950s and 1960s, I did mission work in Mexico, Central America, Jamaica, Barbados and in some of the Bahama Islands. I saw many souls saved on these mission fields.

Since 1972 I have been a full-time evangelist. In these years I have held hundreds of meetings, and I still continue to travel and preach.

This summary is far from complete, but it gives a glimpse of God's blessings through the years and of some of the miracles I have seen Him perform.

Chapter 16

Preaching From the Sky

T here was a time when I made a most unique use of a small plane. In 1948 one of the radio stations carrying my daily broadcast was WFKY in Frankfort, Kentucky. Through the broadcast on that station I became acquainted with Clark Karsner and his family.

Clark was operating a flight school from a small airport on his farm at Monterey, Kentucky, not far from Frankfort. He was training pilots on the GI Bill. Because I owned and flew a plane, and because we were both interested in spreading the Gospel, Clark and I became good friends.

Clark gave considerable support to my radio ministry, and one day he came to me with another idea for spreading the Gospel. He suggested that I preach from an airplane over a powerful loudspeaker.

I was skeptical. I thought that the plane would

pass over an area so quickly that people on the ground would not hear enough of the message for it to have any effect on them. Clark had evidently been in touch with the Lord, and he was convinced that his idea would work.

I had another objection. There was no amplifier being built that had enough power to carry the message from the plane to the ground. Besides, I did not know of a way to power such an amplifier if we had one.

Clark had already looked into that. He had found an electronics engineer who would build a loudspeaker with the needed power, and he would build a power supply from army surplus parts to power it.

Clark offered to pay for the system and have it installed on one of his planes. Then he would fly it every afternoon when the weather was good enough for people to be outside, and he would beam the message down to them.

"How can I ride with you in such an overloaded plane and do the preaching?" I asked.

Clark had an answer for that also. That was before the days of tape recorders, but RCA had come out with a wire recorder. He was sure that we could record the messages on it, and he could play it back over the loudspeaker.

I still was not convinced, but it was his money, and if he wanted to spend it that way, I was willing to go along.

In a short time the electronics man built the loudspeaker, and it was quite a contraption. It looked like we would need a pickup truck to move it. Mounted on the main amplifier were several large radio tubes. The two output tubes were enormous. Also, there was a huge, war-surplus dynamotor to power the amplifier. The army must have used it to power field transmitters during the war. The dynamotor weighed about 75 pounds, and there was a mammoth storage battery, the largest one I had ever seen, to power it. There were two big horns with brackets to bolt them on the wing-struts of the plane. The RCA wire recorder probably weighed another 75 pounds. When all that equipment was loaded in the small Aeronca trainer, there was barely room for Clark to squeeze into his seat beside it. The plane was so overloaded, he had to fly it under an experimental license.

I still wondered if we could reach people in that way, but I went to Clark's home and recorded the first message to be broadcast from The Gospel Plane. Mrs. Karsner played the piano and sang a verse of a song. Then I recorded a two minute sermon.

The following week Clark flew The Gospel Plane to a different town each afternoon, slowed it to the slowest possible flying speed, turned on the loudspeaker and the recorder, and circled as the message blasted down.

The response was immediate and surprising. The next Sunday morning, when I gave the invitation in the church I was pastoring in Lexington, a handsome young farmer came down the aisle and took my hand.

"I have been converted," he began, "and I want to tell the church how I got saved. One day last week, I was working in my barn when I heard singing coming down from above. I ran out of the barn, still carrying the pitchfork I had been using. I looked up and saw that the singing was coming from a small plane, and I stood by the barn door and listened to the message that followed. After the plane was gone, I bowed my head and asked the Lord to save me."

Soon I heard of a man who stopped his truck on the streets of Lexington and stood beside it, listening to the message from The Gospel Plane. He also trusted Jesus as his Saviour. In a village near Lexington, after hearing the message from The Gospel Plane, several people fell on their knees and called on the Lord for salvation. A black man told me how he had heard singing from the air as he worked, laying the walls of a basement for a house. He thought the Lord was coming, and he dropped his tools, ran home, got on his knees, and asked the Lord to save him.

To this day I frequently meet people who tell me that they were saved after hearing the Gospel from the plane. Recently, in a church in Lexington, a lady told me that she had been ironing when she heard the message from the sky and trusted the Lord.

Numbers of people wrote me their impressions of The Gospel Plane. A few of their letters follow.

> I was all but overwhelmed this morning as I sat reading my Bible, when suddenly, out of the blue, I recognized your voice ringing out, *"As it was in the days of Noah."* Oh how we need to hear that message.
>
> With my Bible in my hand, I walked out into the yard and listened, wishing in my heart that I could be up there with you, helping proclaim the Gospel news.
>
> Keep up the good work. I have predicted that you will prove to be a Moody, a Spurgeon, a Sunday, or a Whitfield, Gentleman, Kentucky.

> I heard you the other day as your plane circled over Nicholasville. It brought tears to my eyes . . . I have heard

all kinds of advertising from planes, but never before have I heard the Word of God from a plane, Lady, Kentucky.

I was in Georgetown Tuesday afternoon and heard your airplane and the Gospel message. I told my daughter that's what I call stepping out for Jesus, Lady, Kentucky.

I just have to write after hearing you in the air yesterday. It sounded so good, but it sure put many thoughts in my mind about the last days, Lady, Kentucky.

I think your preaching from the air is the greatest thing I ever heard of. People will hear who have never heard the Gospel in any other way, Man and wife, Kentucky.

Reprint, Lockland Baptist Witness

Louis Arnold owns his private airplane. He not only flies it to and from his engagements in churches, preaching revivals, etc., but now has rigged up his plane with an amplifier and is preaching the Gospel over Lexington, Kentucky and other cities.

I have read about the Devil being *"the prince of the power of the air."* Louis Arnold has accepted the Devil's challenge to the sole right of the air, and is heralding glad tidings of redemptive joy from the ether regions. This is most interesting, since most religious programs have been denied the use of radio.

It will be a miracle if the Devil and his gang do not seek to prevent Brother Arnold from spreading the Gospel as he soars through the air. It will indeed be interesting to know what they could do about it.

More power to the man who rises above the earth's solid surface to preach the Gospel. —Lockland Baptist Witness

----- Ed. Note.

The Lockland Baptist Witness was a paper published by the Lockland Baptist Church while Rev. Ben Hillard was pastor there. Later, Dr. John Rawlings became pastor of the church and led them to buy some of the most beautiful property in the Cincinnati area. Dr. Rawlings built great buildings for the rapidly growing church, renamed it, Landmark Baptist Temple, and pastored there for many years. Landmark Baptist Temple became one of the great churches of the nation under the ministry of Dr. Rawlings.

Because of The Gospel Plane, I was invited by Baptista Films to come to their studios in Wheaton, Illinois to be filmed for a movie, entitled, *Voice From the Sky.* After I made my part of the movie, Baptista Films sent a camera crew and a director to Lexington to finish filming it. For many years the movie was available to churches throughout the United States.

Clark Karsner went home to be with the Lord a few years ago. Now his son, Don, is preaching the Gospel and is a successful pastor.

What a joy it will be when I get home to Heaven and rejoice with Clark and his good wife, his preacher son, and the souls who were saved because of Clark's idea and his faithfulness in flying the plane with the Gospel message.

Chapter 17

Plane Travel Miracles

After flying the J3 Cub for a couple of years, I decided I needed a better plane. I wanted a plane that was faster, seated more than two people, had better instruments, a radio, a heater, and more comfort. All that seemed out of my reach, but I finally found a used Stinson 105 that I could afford. The Stinson seated two people side by side and a third person on a jump seat in the back that was crowded into an enlarged luggage compartment. It had the other things I wanted, but it had one problem; it was underpowered. I bought it anyway.

Being underpowered meant that the plane loved the ground. It used up most of a long runway before I could coax it into the air and drag it over the boundary fence. It was somewhat like a bumblebee. Mathematically speaking, a bumblebee is not supposed to be able to fly. Its body is too heavy for its wing span. The bumble-bee doesn't know that, so it flies anyway. So I did manage to fly my new plane.

I had some good times in that plane, and I had some close calls in it as well. Flying the old J3 Cub had become second nature to me. I could fly it like a bird, and I did things with it that I could never do with another plane, certainly not with the Stinson. I came near killing myself in the Stinson a few times before I learned that. "*. . . But God . . .*"

The Stinson was a beautiful plane, and I had a picture of a flying Bible painted on the side of the fuselage, along with the words, *The Flying Evangelist.*

Close Call Returning From Michigan

One of the closest calls I had in the Stinson was when I flew it to Detroit, Michigan for a revival in the early spring. I landed at the near-est airport to the church where I was to hold the meeting. The field had a graveled runway, and since the spring thaw had not come the ground under the gravel was frozen solid. I had no trouble landing and taxiing to a tie-down where I could secure the plane while I was in the meet-ing.

Two weeks later, when I attempted to take off for the flight home, the ground had started thawing beneath the graveled surface. In Kentucky a thaw starts at the top, but in Michigan the ground thaws below the surface first. Not knowing that, I almost cracked up the plane when I tried to takeoff.

A young man had decided to fly to Lexington with me, and for some reason our departure was delayed until afternoon. When we reached the airport, we loaded our bags in the plane. I had the plane serviced and did the usual inspection. Then the line boy cranked the engine, and I taxied out to takeoff.

At the end of the runway, I turned the plane into the wind and opened the throttle to start my takeoff run. Just as the plane started forward, the thawing ground gave way, and the wheels broke through the gravel into the mud. The propeller blast lifted the tail of the plane off the ground, and it started nosing over. I cut the power instantly. If I had not the plane would have landed on its back.

In spite of my quick action, the tip of the propeller struck the gravel before the tail wheel dropped back on the runway. The propeller was not seriously damaged, but the manager of the airport insisted that I taxi to the shop and let his mechanic check it before I tried to take off again. He got enough help to push the plane out of the mud and to the shop.

There was really nothing wrong with the propeller, but the mechanic sanded a small rough place from it. That delayed my takeoff for a considerable time, and he did not forget to charge for what he had done.

Finally he pronounced the plane safe to fly, and I was directed to a more solid takeoff area. This time I took off without difficulty, but I realized that the delay might keep me from reaching Lexington before dark.

After we were in the air, I encountered a strong head wind. That slowed our progress, and I realized that I could run out of fuel and daylight before we reached Lunkin Airport in Cincinnati where I planned to land and refuel. Even if my fuel lasted, I did not have landing lights, and my radio was almost inoperable.

My instinct told me to fly fast and get as far as I could before dark, but my training told me to slow the airplane to conserve fuel. I pulled back on the throttle enough to slow the engine but not enough to lose flying speed.

I did not tell my passenger that I was worried, but I kept looking for an airport were I could land and refuel, even though my chart indicated that there was no airport along my route. I knew that if I did not find an airport, I might have to make a forced landing in a rough, muddy field, and it would soon be too dark to do that. Frantically I looked for a town large enough to have a small landing field that was not on the chart. Maybe I would just happen to fly over it.

I watched the dropping needle on my gas gauge, and the fading daylight that came into the cockpit from the overcast sky. My nerves were growing more taut by the minute. I knew it was time to pray, and I knew that I must soon make a decision. I must either attempt to land on an unlikely field, or trust my dwindling gas supply to get me to a town with a landing field, maybe Cincinnati.

Not wanting to frighten my passenger, I prayed silently, "Dear Lord, please tell me what to do." I continued to pray as the plane sliced through the gathering gloom. The ground below me was rough and hilly, and there was no field where I could safely land the plane, so I continued to fly.

Night came almost suddenly. It appeared to drop out of the overcast sky and to envelope us. Now the die was cast. I had to keep flying and hoping that my dwindling gas supply would last until I could find a lighted airport.

I switched on the cockpit light and the running lights, knowing that we were in serious trouble. I flew on, watching the gas gauge and the compass. I continued to pray, knowing that only the Lord could guide me to a safe landing.

Before long the fuel gauge was bumping empty, and I listened for any miss in the engine that would signal the last of the fuel. The steady roar of the engine was small comfort, for I knew that soon the roar could become a sputter, and the engine would stop.

Moments later I saw several blinking lights ahead. They were randomly spaced over a wide area, and none of them appeared to be a beacon at a landing field. They did indicate, however, that I was approaching a town, and maybe, just maybe, one of the lights would guide me to a landing field.

I did not have enough fuel to fly to the lights one by one and check them. Perhaps I did not have enough to even fly to one of them. I looked at the gauge. It was still moving—barely. I had to fly towards the right light—if there was a right one.

"Dear Lord, guide me," I prayed. At once I felt impressed to fly toward one of the lights, and I turned the plane in that direction. The light was not a beacon for an airport, I knew, but I continued to fly toward it anyway.

The gas gauge soon stopped moving, but the

engine kept roaring on, boring through the night. Minutes passed, then, miracle of miracles, I saw a concrete runway below me. The light had led me to a runway. If it had been a grass field or blacktop runway I would never have seen it, but the unstained concrete reflected just enough light from the overcast sky for me to see it.

There were no lights around the field, so it must be closed for the night, I concluded. I could not see if there were obstructions, power lines, smokestacks, or tall buildings near the field, so I decided to approach the field higher than normal, line up with the runway, and glide toward it, slightly above landing speed.

When I was sure I had passed any unseen obstructions and crossed the boundary of the field, I would cross the controls on the plane to make it side-slip and lose altitude rapidly. That was a safe enough maneuver in daylight, but it would be tricky in the dark. If I made it safely to the proximity of the runway, I would take the plane out of the slip and try for a landing on a runway I would probably not be able to see.

The engine droned on as I circled the field to line up with the runway. Then suddenly a huge spotlight, near the ground, came on at the end of the runway. It was shining down the runway and straight into my eyes. Almost blinded, I kept going. If my gas would only last, I would fly around behind the light and approach the runway. I prayed that my fuel would last.

The engine droned on and the prop kept turning. When I got behind the light, I had to almost feel my way toward the boundary of the field. I hoped I was high enough to clear any unseen obstructions, and not too high to land after I crossed the boundary. Tension was so thick in the cockpit, I could have sliced it. I knew that I would only have one chance to land on that runway. I had to do this one right.

Time seemed to stand still, but at last I passed the light at the boundary and could see the runway. I was too high, so I cut the throttle and put the plane in a steep side-slip so I would not overshoot the field. I was flying by the seat of my pants, and I could hear the wind slicing past the plane.

The plane slid downward, near a stall, and the runway was coming up too fast. I brought the controls to normal, and the plane righted itself. I dropped the nose slightly, then pulled back on the wheel, feeling the plane slow and settle. A short eternity! Then the wheels bumped the runway. Ah, blessed land. Terra firma!

I turned the plane and taxied toward a building, now visible in the glare of the floodlight.

Two men came out to meet me and my almost forgotten passenger. They pumped our hands, feeling good that they had made it possible for us to make a safe landing.

"We should have been gone long before we heard your plane," one of them said. "We had been closed a long time, but we just kept hanging around talking, something we have never done before."

I don't remember what I told them, but I know that the Lord kept them there to turn the runway light on so I could land. God had performed a miracle to save my life.

Forced Landing in Georgia

While I had the Stinson the Gulf Oil Corporation offered free gas and oil to any private pilot who would fly to the air races in Miami. I signed up for the trip, and agreed to paste the Gulf Oil Company's logo on the cowling of my plane. At that time I had never been to Florida, and, loving flying the way I did, I considered that the chance of a lifetime.

Brother Roy Edwards, a deacon from Salem Baptist Church, where I had pastored years before, went with me. We must have been delayed getting started, for it was midafternoon when we landed in Georgia to refuel.

"Fill both tanks with gas and check the oil,"

I told the man who came to service my plane. "And be sure that the oil cap is firmly seated," I called over my shoulder as Roy and I started inside.

When we returned, I asked the serviceman if he was sure the oil cap was firmly seated, and he assured me that it was. I knew that the plane would throw the oil out if the cap was not tight, but, because it was late, and because we were in a hurry, I did not check behind him.

Roy and I took off. I climbed the plane to cruising altitude, and again headed south. We had not been flying more than half an hour when I noticed that the RPM of the engine was dropping.

Automatically I pulled the carburetor heat on, in case the engine was icing up. At the same instant, I glanced at the instrument panel and saw that there was no oil pressure. Instantly I knew that the serviceman had not tightened the oil cap. Sick at heart, I turned off the ignition, hoping against hope that I had not already ruined the engine.

The propeller stopped turning, and I started looking for a field large enough to land the plane in. It was very quiet in the cockpit. I could hear the wind as the plane cut through it.

"What's wrong?" Roy asked calmly, though

I doubt that he was feeling calm.

"The engine had no oil pressure, so I had to stop it," I told him.

"This is going to be rough, isn't it?" he asked.

"Not really. This won't be much different from a normal landing. I always land with the engine idling, and there are fields large enough to land in down there." I answered, trying to reassure him.

Below me was a grass field large enough to land an airliner in, but it was full of cattle. My landing plane could stampede them, and they might cause me to crash. Even if they didn't stampede, they could damage the plane before I could get oil and takeoff again.

Next to that field was a large, last-year's cornfield. The corn had been picked, but the stalks were still standing. I decided that the stalks would do less damage to the plane than the cows could do, so I circled the cornfield, turned into the wind and lined up with the corn rows. Slowly I glided down and landed. The plane bumped a time or two on the rough ground and rolled to a stop. I looked at Roy and he smiled a weak smile.

We got out and pushed the plane to the end of the field and tied it to the fence. Then we found a phone in a farmhouse and called for help.

We had landed near Albany, Georgia, and

some mechanics from the airport came out and checked the engine. It had to be rebuilt, so they removed it from the plane and took it to their shop.

Roy and I decided to go on to Florida on a bus. We made a tour down one coast and up the other. Then Roy went home, and I returned to Albany to get my plane. Because I had been careless, I was a wiser and a poorer man when I flew home from Albany.

A Stall Almost Killed Me

The forced landing in Georgia was child's play compared to what happened to me on a winter day when I attempted to fly from Lexington to Louisville for an evangelistic conference.

That morning I phoned the weather bureau and inquired about flying conditions. They told me there was nothing to be concerned about, though they were expecting some widely-scattered snow flurries.

Reassured, I drove to Cool Meadow Airport, where the Stinson was based. I got the plane out of the hanger and had it serviced. This time, of course, and all future times, I personally saw that the oil cap and the gas caps were properly seated. Then I ran my preflight inspection, started the plane, and taxied out for takeoff.

Because of the underpowered engine, I used

most of the grass runway before I lifted the plane into the air. I cleared the trees beyond the boundary fence, then dropped the nose, as I had to with that plane, to let it gain flying speed. Just then a blinding snowstorm closed around me, and I could not see beyond the windshield.

Fear stabbed at me as I remembered the radio station tower directly ahead of me. Instinctively, I pulled back on the control wheel to climb over the tower.

An airplane in flight has its own center of gravity, so with the ground not visible, I had no way of knowing the attitude of the plane, whether it was flying level, climbing, turning or diving. I had blind flight instruments, but I was not trained to use them. I did not even think to look at them. My only thought was to get over the tower.

Speed is what makes a plane fly. If the speed drops below flying speed, the plane stalls and starts toward the ground nose first. It can even get in a spin and spin to the ground like a corkscrew.

When I pulled back on the wheel, the Stinson stalled. I heard the engine roaring louder than usual, and, in panic, I realized that I was in a dive—straight toward the ground with only two or three hundred feet to go. I glanced at the airspeed indicator and saw that I was doing 140 MPH, and the airspeed was climbing. The tachometer was past the red danger mark and climbing. I knew I had only seconds before crashing into the ground—and sudden death.

"Lord save me," I prayed.

At that instant it felt as if God's hands were controlling my hands. Then I felt the plane pull-out of the dive, and I felt as if I were going through the seat. I feared that the wings would break off the plane, and that it would disintegrate in the air. "*. . . But God.*"

The plane stayed together, and it had plenty of speed to climb. I looked at the blind flight instruments and used the little knowledge I had of them to keep the plane flying safely. When I had reached a safe altitude, I turned the plane, ever so gently. I did what pilots call a 180 and flew out of the snow squall. I flew back to the airport and landed. Then I got on my knees and thanked the Lord for saving my life. I still praise Him for saving my life that day and for letting me live all these years to preach the Gospel.

Chapter 18

A New Church is Born

In the winter of 1949 I rented Clay Gentry Arena in Lexington, Kentucky on Sundays and started holding afternoon services there. The arena was filled from the beginning and numbers were converted in the services. I tried to get the converts to join one of the local Baptist churches but was unsuccessful. A preacher friend told me that when he caught fish he did not leave them on the bank to die but put them on a string. He convinced me that I should organize a church for my converts to join.

In the spring I rented some classrooms in the old Johnson School building in Lexington at the corner of Fourth and Limestone and started having Sunday school classes in the smaller rooms and services in the largest room.

People continued to be saved, and the first Sunday in August I organized Fellowship Baptist Church with 70 charter members. Others were awaiting baptism, and the first official act of the church was to baptize them.

By the following spring the membership had reached 200, and we were so crowded in the classroom we asked for and received permission from the owner of the building to remove some walls and make an auditorium that would seat 700 people.

We moved into the newly enlarged auditorium on Mother's Day and had services morning, afternoon, and evening. The new auditorium was packed for all three services.

After the morning service we had dinner on the ground, and during the time of fellowship a man told me that he wanted to donate a hundred dollars toward the purchase of a tent for me to use in revivals. I thanked him and told him that I was not planning to hold tent revivals that summer, because I was going to be busy with the new church. That night we started a revival in the new auditorium.

Johnson School Burned

I had set up a broadcasting studio in Johnson School, and the next morning, as I was getting ready to go to the broadcast my phone rang, and one of my men told me that Johnson School was on fire. I jumped in my car and drove across town as fast as traffic permitted. I doubt that I paid any attention to the speed limit.

By the time I reached Johnson School firemen had the fire under control, but the building was smoke-filled and dripping with water. In spite of that some of the men of the church and I were able to get most of our equipment out of the building. I preached outside that night beside the still smoking building.

The next day I phoned the man who had offered to give a hundred dollars toward the purchase of a tent and told him that Johnson School had burned, and that I was going to have to buy a tent to hold services in until we could find a location and build.

A New Location Found Us

A day or two after the fire a Christian real estate man contacted me and said that he had found some property for sale that would be a good location for our church. I told him that we had no money. In fact we were worse than broke, but he insisted that I go with him to see the property anyway.

He took me further out North Limestone Street than where we had been meeting, and turned into a drive that led up to a large, weatherboarded, unoccupied house. He showed me through the house, and we walked over some overgrown ground behind the house with some decaying chicken houses on it.

I saw that when the chicken houses were cleared away there would be room for a Gospel tent with parking around it, and there was room to build a church in front of the house.

The real estate agent told me the price of the property, and we discussed the terms. He was sure that the people who owned the property would let us buy it with a small amount down and monthly payments. I told him I would discuss it with the membership of the church the next Sunday and let him know.

The next Sunday morning we met at Fourth and Limestone and had services in the open-air. After the service I told the people that I wanted to show them something, and that I wanted them to follow me in their cars.

Most of them followed me to the property the real estate agent had showed me. We all parked and got out, and I showed them around. Then I stood on the front steps of the house, and they gathered around me.

"We can buy this property to build our church on," I told them.

"I make a motion that we buy it," one of the men said, and someone seconded the motion. No one asked the price of the property or how we could pay for it. I asked for a show of hands and everyone voted to buy the property. They were as convinced as I was that it was God's will for us to buy it.

A Tent Provided

We soon took possession of the property, and a number of the men and I spent some days tearing down the old chicken houses and cleaning away the debris. I knew that we had to have a tent to meet in while we were building, but I only had a hundred dollars toward the purchase.

After we finished clearing the ground some of the men and I met to discuss buying a new tent. I told them what a new tent would cost, and we agreed to order it and try to raise the money for it by the time it arrived.

I picked up the phone to place the order, but the Holy Spirit told me to put the phone down. I put the phone in the cradle, and one of my men asked why I did not place the call.

"I just heard from Heaven," I told him. "Next week I am going to Wheaten, Illinois to make a film for Baptista Films, and the Lord just told me that while I am there He is going to give me a tent for a hundred dollars."

I'm not sure the men believed that I had heard from Heaven, but they agreed to wait about ordering a tent.

The next week I flew my plane to Wheaton, and went to Baptista Films. After I finished making my part of a film entitled, *Voice From the Sky*, I asked the Lord where I was to go to get the tent. At that time Dr. John R. Rice had his headquarters in Wheaton, and I felt led to go to see him. Surely he would know someone who had a tent to sell.

When I reached Dr. Rice's office his secretary told me that he was out of town. She suggested that I talk with his son-in-law, Walt Hansford, instead.

Walt and I exchanged greetings and talked briefly. "What can I do for you?" he then asked.

"I'm looking for a used tent to buy. Our church has burned, and we need a tent to meet in until we can build," I told him.

"I own a half interest in a tent," he said. "I am willing to sell, but I have to call my partner."

He made the call, and I could tell from the conversation that his partner was also willing to sell.

"How much?" I heard Walt asked.

I knew how much they would ask for the tent before he told me.

"One hundred dollars," Walt said as he hung up the phone.

"Ship it to me, freight collect," I told him.

The next Sunday, in an open-air service at Fourth and Limestone, I told the people that I had bought a tent for a hundred dollars, and that we would put it up on our property when it arrived.

The tent arrived the next week. It was well-worn, but there was great excitement when we put it up. We had three services in the tent the next Sunday, and it was filled for every service. We continued to have three services every Sunday, and the tent overflowed in almost every one of them. The tent served us well, but we knew that we had to build before cold weather arrived.

The Bank President Changes His Mind

A vice president of First National Bank agreed to loan our church the money we needed to pay off the original loan on our property so we could get a deed. The time was set for me and our treasurer to close with the people we owed and their attorney at two o'clock in the afternoon.

That morning I went to the office of the vice president who had promised to loan us the money, and he met me with a long face.

"The president of the bank has vetoed your loan," he told me. I thanked him and went to the office of the president of the bank and explained to him why we needed the loan.

"You are not going to get a loan here," he

said bluntly.

"I do business in this bank; my church does business here, and we would like to have our loan here," I told him.

"You're not going to get a loan in this bank," he said emphatically, and he got up and walked impatiently back and forth in front of his desk.

There was nothing more I could say, so I thanked him and left. I went to my car and prayed. I explained to the Lord, as if He didn't know, that we needed the money to close on our property and that I didn't have much time to get it. There was not time to negotiate with another bank, and they probably would have turned us down anyway. "What can I do?" I asked the Lord.

At once there came to my mind a millionaire farmer who raised racehorses. I had never met him, but I felt led to go to his home and ask him to sign the note, along with my trustees, for the loan we needed from First National Bank.

I drove to the home of the millionaire, and he answered the door when I rang the bell. I think the Lord had him waiting for me. I introduced myself, and he invited me to come in. I explained my problem to him and said, "Mr. _____, I need you to sign the note, along with my trustees, for a loan at First National Bank. The president of the bank has turned us down.

Without hesitation he said, "I'm one of the trustees in that bank. I will not sign for the entire amount of your loan, but I will sign for a thousand dollars. That should do it."

He picked up the phone, called the bank, and asked to speak with the president. When the president came on the line he spoke with him briefly and hung up the phone.

"The papers will be ready for you to sign when you get back to the bank," he said. I thanked him, hurried back to the bank, and went to the president's office. The papers were ready for me and my trustees to sign. That was a small miracle for God, but it was a big miracle for me.

Ground Breaking for the Church

By the time we had our ground breaking in July the membership of the church had grown to 300, but our faith was larger than our membership. We decided to build the largest auditorium the zoning board would allow us to build on our property. That turned out to be a building that an estimated 2 thousand people could crowd into.

The rest of the summer we were busy winning souls, getting the walls of our building up, and raising money to pay for it. We knew we had to get the building up before cold weather.

The church was a miracle from the beginning, and so many miracles occured when we were building our auditorium that people started calling it, "Miracle Auditorium."

Steel Provided for Building

When the walls were almost up our builder told us we should place the order for the steel beams to span the 100 foot wide auditorium. We placed the order, and a couple of weeks later I received a letter from the steel company telling me that the government had frozen all steel sales for domestic use because of the Korean War. They were going to place our order on file, and they would get in touch with us as soon as the government released the restriction.

The following Sunday, when the people met in the tent for the morning service, I read the letter to them and asked if anyone had any suggestion about what we should do.

Someone who had more faith than I did said, "Why don't we pray?" That sounded like a good idea, so I agreed that we should pray. At once the people started coming down the saw-dust covered aisles and kneeling. They knelt at the front, in the aisles, and on the ground outside the tent. We prayed, then continued with the services.

One morning, about two weeks later, when I arrived at the building site I saw a crew unloading steel from a big eighteen-wheel truck.

I parked my car and joined some men who had collected to watch. Soon the pastor from a nearby church joined us. After a moment he said to me. "We have had an order in for steel for our church for over two years, and we cannot get any assurance about when we can get it. You must know somebody at the top."

"We do," I told him. We had gone all the way to the top when we asked God to intervene and send us the steel we needed. Our God is a God of miracles.

Miracle Weather

By the time the roof was on the church and the doors and windows were in place, it was getting too cold to stay in the tent, so we installed some gas heaters along the walls of the unfinished building and moved in. The heaters did not do an adequate job, and the dirt floor was cold, but it was better that being in the tent. It is amazing that people continued to attend services under those conditions, but they did.

January brought very cold weather, and the dirt floor became unbearably cold. We felt that if we could pour a concrete floor that would be an improvement.

The contractor told me that he would need two weeks of above freezing weather to pour the ten thousand square feet of floor in our auditorium. I told the people what he had said, and we started praying for two weeks of dry, above freezing weather.

I announced that we were praying for two

weeks of dry, above freezing weather on my daily radio program. A vice president of the First National Bank heard the announcement and told people that we would get the weather we needed, because we always got what we prayed for. Sure enough, the weather turned warm, and we had two weeks of dry, above freezing weather. We got our concrete floor finished and continued to worship in our unfinished building.

Miracle Growth

Fellowship Baptist Church was a miracle church. People drove to the services every Sunday from every adjoining county. When we finally finished our auditorium an estimated 4 thousand tried to attend the dedication. Traffic was tied up for two miles in every direction. It was impossible to park all the cars, and half of the people could not have got in the building if they had reached it.

We continued to have three services every Sunday, and we often had special meetings. The building was often filled and sometimes so many people attended that many sat on the floor or stood around the walls. People continued to be saved, and the church continued to grow.

One Night Revival

Before the building was finished, I invited Dr. B. R. Lakin to come for one of his famed "One Night Revivals." He was then pastor of Cadle

Tabernacle in Indianapolis, and most everyone listened to his daily broadcast over WLW in Cincinnati. I wrote the service we had up in our paper under the title, *Miracle Night at Miracle Auditorium.* I quote a part of the article.

When I arrived for the service I had to park several blocks from the auditorium. Our parking lot was filled and every street and every cross street was parked solid for many blocks in every direction.

When I reached the auditorium I found it jammed and packed, and many people were outside trying to get in. It was a struggle to get to the platform. Every seat was taken, and every aisle was jammed with people standing as close as they could together from the front to the back. Every available inch in the large choir was taken, and the side rooms were packed. The rooms in the house at the back were packed with people who would listen to the service on the loudspeaker.

When Dr. Lakin came to bring his message, the power of God was upon him. For more than an hour people sat spellbound and listened to the greatest

Gospel message they had ever heard.

When the invitation was given it was more wonderful still. People were asked to crowd to each side of the crowded aisles. That made a narrow, almost impassable passageway. Normally in such crowded conditions it is difficult to get people to come forward, but that was not so on this night. More than a hundred pressed their way forward to trust Christ as Saviour.

At the close of the service people expressed a desire, with a show of hands and prolonged applause, for Dr. Lakin to return to our auditorium at any time he felt led to do so. We praise God for a Miracle Night at Miracle Auditorium.

Chapter 19

Mission Work in the Islands

After I had been in the ministry for some years, it occurred to me that few evangelists were holding meetings on mission fields. We were sending out all kinds of missionaries, other than evangelists, to mission fields. We were sending medical missionaries, educational missionaries, pastoral missionaries, construction missionaries, and so on. That is no longer true. Many evangelists now travel to foreign lands and hold meetings. Anyway, I felt that the Lord wanted me to hold meetings on mission fields, and for a number of years I held meetings in at least one foreign country each year. The Lord greatly blessed these meetings. I do not remember ever giving an invitation in a foreign country without people being saved.

One of the most fruitful fields I visited was the Bahama Islands. My first meeting there was at the invitation of my missionary friend, Rev. Robert Neighbour. He invited me to come and bring my tent for a revival at West End, Grand Bahama.

Brother Neighbour had not had any experience with Gospel tents, so he could not have anticipated what would be involved in getting the tent and equipment to the island. I had to load the tent, with all the poles, iron stakes, ropes, electric wire, lights, public address equipment, and seat ends on a two ton truck and haul it from Lexington, Kentucky to West Palm Beach, Florida. From there, he told me we could ship the tent and equipment to West End on a small ship.

In due time I arrived in West Palm Beach with all the equipment on my truck. Eight of my church members went with me, two of the men riding with me in the truck, and the others riding in a car. Brother Neighbour had made arrangements for our party to stay in West Palm Beach overnight.

To my dismay he told me that the boat he was going to ship the tent on had left early, and we would have to make other arrangements. He thought we could ship the tent and equipment to the island on the airline we were to travel on. I thought not. Nonetheless, the next morning we all arrived at the airport in two cars and my truck shortly before flight time.

At that time the only airline flying regularly scheduled flights from Florida to the Bahamas was Midet Airline, a small company that was flying DC-3 planes. The DC-3 was a two-motor, prop-driven aircraft that seated twenty-one passengers.

It is impossible to describe the reaction of the people at Midet Airlines when ten adults and three or four babies and children showed up, almost late, with their luggage, boxes of groceries, calculated to last a week, and all the tent equipment I had on the truck. Saying that they were fit to be tied is putting it mildly.

When the baggage handlers looked in our truck and saw the tent, five big bags of it, wire, poles, stakes, lumber, PA system, recorder, podium, songbooks, iron seat ends, and other items too numerous to mention, they almost went into orbit.

The entire organization, from the president of the company to the people who loaded the plane, were in turmoil. They threw up their hands in disbelief. There was no way they could fly all that load to West End on their airline. They didn't have that kind of cargo space.

After much discussion and head shaking, another person went out to take a look in the truck. It may have been the president of the company, for all I know. It is a wonder he did not have a heart attack on the spot. He went back to his office shaking his head. We followed and waited while he talked it over with his people.

Brother Neighbour should have been a diplomat. Somehow he pacified the airline people and persuaded them to take us and our baggage and equipment to West End, though they said they could not take the iron stakes. We would have to cut wood stakes on the island. And they could only take part of the tent this trip. They would bring the rest of the tent on the next flight, two days later.

Finally, with half of the tent and equipment, loaded, we all got on the airplane and headed for the island. After a short overwater flight of eighty-five miles, the plane nosed down for a landing at West End.

I looked out at the island and saw the runway, and a spontaneous prayer rose to my lips. "Lord, give me this island for Christ," I prayed, and I believed that He was going to do it.

After more than the usual hubbub of deplaning, collecting baggage, passing through customs, and getting transportation to West End, a village on the west end of the island, we reached the two story house where Brother Neighbour had arranged for our party to stay.

With considerable effort we unloaded all we had brought with us and stowed the part of the tent and equipment we had brought on a side porch. The rest of our paraphernalia we carried inside. Then I set forth to find a place to pitch the tent. Imagine my consternation when I found that the island was almost solid rock. There was no way we could drive wooden stakes in the ground. Greatly disappointed, I returned to the house.

It was now well past noon, and the ladies in our party were stirring about in the groceries we had brought, trying to decide what to fix for our lunch. About that time one of the men came in with some fish he had bought from someone. I volunteered to clean the fish and took them down to the seaside and started cleaning them.

Soon a native lady approached me and asked, "Are you a preacher?"

"Yes, I'm a preacher," I replied. I had no idea why she thought I was a preacher.

"What kind of preacher are you?" she asked.

"I'm a good preacher," I teased.

"I don't mean that. What denomination are you?"

"I'm a Baptist."

"Me too," she smiled. "Will you preach for us tonight?"

"Where will I preach?"

"You can preach in the lodge hall. Our church has services there on Sundays."

"How will the people know I'm going to preach?"

"We'll tell them, and they'll come. You'll see."

"All right. I'll be glad to preach for you."

Revival at West End

That night the lodge hall was packed, and I started one of the greatest revivals I have ever had. We had people saved in every service. Often there were many professions in a service. There was great excitement and much joy. Many of the converts testified of the great change that had come into their lives.

The meeting lasted a week, and we were to leave for Florida on the noon plane on Monday. I held the last service of the meeting that morning at ten o'clock.

The school dismissed their classes so the students could attend that service, and most all the other people at West End attended. The lodge hall was packed to overflowing, and great numbers of people filled the yard and stood along the road that ran past the lodge hall.

After preaching, I gave an invitation, and at once people started coming to the front of the building and falling on their knees. Soon there was no room at the front, and they started kneeling in the aisles. Soon there was no room in the aisles. I looked out through the windows and saw people on their knees on all sides of the building. I cannot even guess how many people were converted that day. The following testimonies I recorded will give some idea of the results of the meeting.

Testimonies of Converts

One young man said, "I am happier than I ever was in all my life."

A lady said, "I have never had such joy in my heart."

Another said, "Thank you, thank you, thank you, thank you, for coming to our island to preach."

Another said, "We would like to keep you in our island forever."

An elderly man said, "This is the greatest thing that has come to this island in my lifetime."

Another said, "We have never had such meetings as these, and we feel that this is God's last warning to these islands."

A lady said, "It is going to make our island a little heaven on earth."

One of the people told me the name of the only known thief at West End and made it clear that they had no respect for him. Soon after that I met the man they said was a thief on the road. I stopped him, and made an effort to win him to Christ. He said he was not interested, so I placed my hand on his shoulder and prayed for him. Later I was told that he said: "I like that Father Arnold. He met me in the middle of the road and blessed me."

Testimony of An Old Man

On a visit to West End a year later, an old man saw me walking by the sea and called me to his side.

"I want to talk with you," he began when I reached him. "This island is a different place since you were here last year. People used to be unhappy, but they are happy now. They have stopped swearing and started singing. They go about singing, *Jesus Never Fails.*

"I am different too. Before I was saved, I used to worry, but I don't worry anymore. I don't have a pension or Social Security, such as you have in the States, but the Lord is taking care of me.

He proceeded to tell me how he was living from his garden, his few chickens, gifts from friends, and the sale of conch shells to tourists.

His talk reminded me of the testimony of the Psalmist. *"I have been young, and now am old; yet have I not seen the righteous forsaken, nor his seed begging bread"* (Psalms 37:25).

The testimony of the old man inspired me to write the following poem.

God Will Supply

A gray old man lived all alone
Without a thing to call his own.
When someone asked how he got by,
"I trust in God," was his reply.

I once was young, I now am old.
God will supply, I've oft been told.
God will supply, He feeds the birds.
I've read it in His holy Word.

"But aren't you lonely?" someone
asked.
"And don't you tire from all your
tasks?"
"My God is near," was his reply.
"He meets all needs, so I'll get by."

"But what when summer's flowers fade,
And no one comes to give you aid?"
"God cares for me," was his reply.
"His Word can't fail, so I'll get by."

The following year, after a second visit to West End, I wrote in *The Arnold Report:*

Since our first campaign in the Bahamas last March, the work has continued to go steadily forward. You cannot be on the island long without meeting converts from the meeting. The young man who drives one of the two taxicabs at West End was converted in the meeting. Girls who serve in the dining room at the hotel at Butler's Village, and the women who clean the rooms were converted. Men who run the fishing boats were converted. On every hand I met converts, all of them testifying of their conversions, and, at the slightest opportunity, telling what God has done in their lives.

This is only a small accounting of all that God did on this one island. After that meeting I returned to it for meetings again and again, and God always blessed with outstanding results.

Chapter 20

Other Meetings in the Islands

Service at High Rock

I was invited to preach in other places on Grand Bahama Island, and God blessed with good results in all of them.

I preached one night in a small church at Eight Mile Rock. The pastor told me that he only had 40 members. God blessed the service that night, and there were more than 40 converts added to the church. It was no small miracle to see a church more than double in membership in one service.

Outdoor Service at Pine Ridge

Half way up the length of the island there was a lumber camp called Pine Ridge. The lumber company had built a stone church building for the people to use, and both the white and black people worshiped in it.

After I had preached in the church building several times, the man who ran the company's general merchandise store decided that I could reach more people if I preached in the open air. So he had a platform built in front of the store, with a podium and an amplifier on it.

The night I was to preach the people did not start coming until it was almost dark. After that they came and came until there was hardly standing room for them. They gathered on all sides of the platform, some of them close to it and others so far away I could hardly see them in the gathering gloom.

As I preached that night I kept turning around and around so I could preach to all the people. Most of the multitude was made up of men, and when I finished preaching and gave the invitation, they started coming forward at once. They knelt around the platform until there was no room for them. Others knelt behind them, and others behind them. Men were kneeling in the darkness as far as I could see.

Those kneeling started sobbing and praying aloud, and the ones near the platform almost shook it off of its foundation. I have no idea how many were saved that night. I only know that I counted 50 men kneeling near the platform. The open-air service at Pine Ridge was a miracle service.

Services at Water Cay

One of the most unusual experiences I had in the Bahama Islands was the time I went to Water Cay to preach. It is interesting how I happened to go to this island.

Some of the natives either have a strong intuition or they are very sensitive to the leading of the Holy Spirit. I became aware of this during my first trip to Grand Bahama. The first night of the meeting there a man traveled thirty miles in a small sailboat, arriving on Grand Bahama in time for the service. He came to where we were staying to see me that night after the service.

"Today I was out fishing, and I suddenly felt that I should quit fishing and go home and dress and come to Grand Bahama," he began. "When I found the meeting going on tonight, I knew why I had to come." I led him to the Lord that night.

After that, every time I went to Grand Bahama he showed up. And every time he asked me to go to Water Cay, his home island, to preach. Each time I told him I would be glad to go, but he always said, "No, I can't ask you to go. You would have to go in a small sailboat. The sea would be rough, and you would get wet. "

At last one day, he told me that he had arranged a way for me to go. I was to go to the other end of Grand Bahama by taxi. A larger sailboat than the one he usually used would take me from there to Water Cay in sheltered waters.

Rev. Roy Harrison, now deceased, was in our

party at Grand Bahama on that occasion, and he volunteered to go with me to Water Cay.

We traveled up the island as planned, and from there we set sail with a crew of three or four men, including the one who had arranged the trip. We sailed on a calm, crystal-blue sea all day, and late in the afternoon we saw a small hill that appeared to rise out of the sea. At once the men in the boat started pointing and saying, "Water Cay! See? Water Cay! See?"

As we drew near we saw a small harbor, pressed against an island that sloped up from the sea. A great number of people were gathered along the shore.

"Why are all the people here?" I asked.

"They are here to meet you." one of the men said.

"How did they know I was coming?"

"They heard it on the radio."

Water Cay, I soon learned, was one of the most primitive of the islands. There were no automobiles, no highways, no bicycles, and no electricity, but the people did have battery-powered radios. That morning, before we left Grand Bahama, someone called the radio station at Nassau, on New Providence Island, by radio telephone, and asked them to announce that I was going to Water Cay to preach. The radio station had broadcast the message, and the people on Water Cay had heard it.

That day none of the men on Water Cay went out fishing, though that was the way they made their living. Instead they waited on the island all day for me to arrive.

Their 94-year-old pastor was also waiting on the shore to meet me. Later he told me that I was the second preacher to visit his church from the outside during his pastorate of 70 years.

When our boat docked Brother Harrison and I disembarked on one of the most beautiful islands I have ever seen. A pathway, lined with seashells, paved with sand, and shaded by tropical trees, led up from the sea to a village. The natives took our bags, camera, and recorder, leaving us with nothing to carry. They led us along the path, past intersecting paths, to a thatched hut, and the old pastor came along.

"This is your motel," the man who had invited me explained as he led us inside the hut. The hut contained only a bed, a chair, and a dresser. I learned later that a family had moved out so we could stay in the hut that was their home.

The natives placed our equipment and bags in the hut, then led us across the path to another hut and motioned us into it. It contained only a table and two chairs. Another family had moved out so we would have a place to eat.

"What would you favor for your dinner?" the man who had invited me asked.

"Anything you have will be all right," I told him.

He then insisted that we go with him and some others to see their church while the meal was being prepared. We walked with the people and the pastor a quarter mile to their church.

The church was a modest frame building, but I have never seen people who were more proud of their church. They took us inside and showed us the pews and the pulpit, with two chairs and a podium. Then they took us outside and showed us the church bell. It was mounted on a low post about three feet above the ground. The bell was cracked all the way down on one side, and it only clanked when they rang it. Later I was able to get a beautiful brass bell from a railroad train and ship it to them.

When we returned to our dining room, they served us fried Spam, pigeon peas, (native beans that grow on a tree), and maybe some fruit. We ate and returned to our "motel." We rested briefly, then dressed and started to church.

The paths were crowded with people, also going to church. The church was crowded when we arrived, and people kept pressing their way in until there was standing room only. We were told later that every person on the island except one blind man attended the service.

What a service we had! The people sang as only they can sing. Brother Harrison gave a brief testimony. The pastor gave a brief message, and I preached. The power of God was present. There was shouting. There was rejoicing, and people got saved.

The next morning, the people were up early. Someone cooked us a good breakfast. We ate and thanked them. Then we went out and found that the people were going all over the island to gather souvenirs for us to take back with us. While they were doing that, two of the men gave us a demonstration of how they handmade rope from a tropical plant called a sisal.

Soon it was time to go, for we had a long journey back across the sea and down Grand Bahama to West End. The wind had changed, and we had to cross to the other side of the island so we could board the boat in calm water.

We told the people good-bye and started on our way. To my surprise, everyone, including the old pastor, walked with us. About a mile on the way he excused himself, saying that he had not been feeling well for a few days, but the rest of the people continued with us.

We had been walking on level ground, but we soon went down into a kind of a natural amphitheater that was bounded by tropical growth on every side. There the people paused and started singing. We listened, enthralled. After the song, they asked that we preach to them. We preached, prayed, told them good-bye again, and started on. They all continued with us all the way to the sea.

There they stopped and sang again. Then they asked that we preach again. Once again I preached, prayed and told them good-bye.

We got in the boat and thrust off, and the people on the shore started singing, *God be with you till we meet again.* They were still singing when we sailed out of hearing. If they could have walked on the water, I believe they would have gone all the way to Grand Bahama with us.

Visit to Bimini

A few years later Mrs. Arnold and I moved to Florida so we could fly to the islands in the plane the Lord had provided. We had a most unusual experience on a weekend before Christmas. Instead of going to our usual mission point at West End, we flew to Bimini to assess the need for mission work there.

Early in the morning we took off from Fort

Pierce, where we were living, and flew down the Florida coast to Fort Lauderdale. There we landed and refueled. Then we took off for Bimini, some sixty-five miles off the Florida coast. I climbed the plane to 8,000 feet, so we would have considerable glide distance in case of engine failure, then we watched the Florida coast fade in the distance behind us. For a short time we were out of sight of land. That was the critical part of the flight, and we did not breathe easy until we saw the coast of Bimini dimly outlined in the distance.

Shortly after that we were gliding down to the runway for a landing on Bimini. We landed, got out of the plane and tied it down. The only way to get to the village on Bimini was to ferry a short distance across an emerald-blue bay, so we caught the ferry.

We were hungry when we reached the village, and we stopped at a restaurant for a bite to eat. While we were eating, we asked some native boys if there was a Baptist church on the island.

"Yes there is. It's on the far end of the island. "Rev. Smith is the pastor," one of them said.

We finished eating, found lodging, and checked in. Then we walked up the island and found Pastor Smith's home.

He invited us in, and we sat down to get acquainted and to talk of the Lord's work in the islands and especially of his work on Bimini.

"What kind of church do you have, Brother Smith?" I inquired.

"I have a good church," he replied. "I have 300 good members."

"What do you mean, good members?"

"I mean that they are good Christians. They do not drink. They do not gamble. They do not use bad language. They do not run around. Come to church tomorrow and you will see."

The next morning we arrived early at the church and attended the most amazing Sunday school I had ever attended. Even though it was the Sunday before Christmas the church was filled with people. The pastor made us welcome, and we sat with him while the Sunday school superintendent conducted the opening service.

The dark faces of the people were radiant. The superintendent had the happiest, most radiant face I have ever seen. The glory of God seemed to radiate from him.

While he was conducting the service, from time to time the people broke into singing, *"O come, let us adore Him, O come, let us adore Him, O come, let us adore Him, Christ the Lord."* They continued to break into song again and again throughout the Sunday school hour. Each time the song rose higher and higher in praise and adoration until I wanted to prostrate myself at the feet of our precious Saviour.

At one point the pastor leaned over and said, "The people are full of joy because all this week we have been getting ready for Christmas. Each morning they have come to church at four o'clock to pray for an hour. Then they have gone home for breakfast and for the duties of the day. This morning they also came to church at four o'clock and prayed for an hour. Then they went home for breakfast. Now they are back for Sunday school and church, and they are filled with the Spirit."

I felt that for the first time I was learning how to celebrate Christmas.

The church was packed for the morning preaching service, and, as in the Sunday school hour, the people interrupted the service from time to time by singing, *"O come, let us adore Him."* They sung with a spirit of reverence and worship, and, though they interrupted the order of the service, their singing never seemed out of order.

At one point during the service the pastor whispered to me, "Have you noticed that there are a few people seated on the two back pews?"

"Yes," I said, after noticing that those pews were not packed as the others were.

"Those pews are my goat pen," the pastor said.

I looked at him, puzzled, wondering what he meant.

"When any of our members have done something wrong, they have to sit in the goat pen until they get right with the Lord and confess before the church. After that, they can again sit with the rest of the congregation."

Strangely that seemed to work for him. That morning after he preached some of his wayward members came forward to make things right with God and get out of the goat pen. Others came forward for salvation.

Brother Smith preached a good sermon, but that is not what I remember most about the service. To this day, I cannot forget how the people sang again and again, "O *come, let us adore Him, Christ, the Lord.*"

Both morning and evening, when the service ended, the people did not soon leave the building, nor did they begin to visit with each other. Instead they arose and stood in the aisles and around the walls of the auditorium, singing, *"O come, let us adore Him."*

After I preached that night, they sang as they

had in the morning. When they finally decided to go home, they continued to sing as they left the building and turned homeward.

Little groups turned on different pathways, still singing. I watched their flickering lights moving through the pine and palm trees, and I listened to patches of song, floating across the island from every direction, and gradually fading in the distance. *"O come, let us adore Him, . . . O come let us adore Him."*

The voices were at last lost in the distance, but, even after the passing of the years, their message of praise and worship remains strong in my memory.

Chapter 21

Guidance Over the Ocean

In 1959 I decided to fly to some of the southern Bahama Islands that I had not visited before. On that trip I planned to fly to Nassau, land there and refuel, then fly on to the next island, refuel again, then on to the next island, and the next, until I reached my destination. The flight would be over more ocean than I had ever flown over before, so I spent much time planning for the trip and securing the equipment I would need, such as a life raft, life jackets, and cans to carry extra gasoline.

In March Mrs. Arnold and I, and Brother Earl Vanwinkle, one of my preacher boys, took off from West Palm Beach, Florida to fly to Nassau on New Providence Island. As was my practice when flying over water, I climbed the plane to 8 thousand feet so I could see the Florida coast as long as possible. I knew that after I lost sight of Florida it would be some time before I could see the coast of New Providence Island.

The sun was shining when we took off from Florida, but after an hour of flying the sky became overcast. As I flew on it started raining and the visibility decreased until I could hardly tell the sea from the horizon. It was possible that I would not be able to find New Providence Island. I knew that I could fly past it, run out of gas and have to ditch in the ocean. Realizing the danger, I decided to turn back to Florida and try again another day.

As I flew toward Florida the visibility improved enough for me to see the ocean, and I could tell that the wind was blowing huge waves against the path of my flight. That meant that I was bucking a strong head wind, and it was possible that I would run out of gas before I reached the landing field at West Palm Beach.

I knew that north of our path of flight there was a circle of islands called Abaco, and I decided to turn toward them. Surely I would find one of those islands, and perhaps I could land there on a sandy beach.

The weather improved as I flew toward the string of islands. For that I was thankful. That would make it possible for me to see better when I attempted to make a forced landing on a beach.

After I turned north, I knew that the head wind was now a crosswind. Silently I prayed that it would not blow us beyond the islands and out to sea. If that happened I would run out of gas. We would have to ditch in the sea, and it was possible that we would never be found.

As the plane roared on the weather continued to improve. I was glad for that would make it easier for me to find an island where I could land. I flew on, straining to see anything that looked like land. I prayed silently, for I knew we were not out of danger.

Finally, the dim outline of an island came into view, and I relaxed and offered a prayer of thanksgiving. Surely I could find a sandy beach where I could land. A short time later I saw a long concrete runway directly in front of our path of flight. God had guided me straight to that runway.

I circled the airport, lined up with the runway, and landed. I taxied to some buildings on the field, and a man came out to meet us.

"Where are we?" I asked.

"You are at Marsh Harbour," he responded.

I had landed on the largest island in the Abaco chain.

"I know someone here," Mrs. Arnold exclaimed. "I met a student from here when I was in Bob Jones University. His name is Woodis Key."

"Maybe we can find him I suggested."

We went through customs, a minor inconvenience on this island. Then we went to the village to look for Woodis Key.

We soon located his home, and his mother came to the door and welcomed us. We asked for Woodis, and she told us that he was not at home. He had gone out in his boat fishing and would not be home for several days. We thanked her and returned to the village to find something to eat.

While we were eating, to our surprise, Woodis entered the restaurant and came to our table. He and Mrs. Arnold exchanged greetings and she introduced him to me and Brother Vanwinkle.

"I was out fishing this morning, and I had an impression that I ought to come home. Now I know why," he said.

While we finished eating we told Woodis how we happened to be there.

"I believe God send you," he said. "Our church has been praying for someone to come and hold a revival for us."

We concluded that God had sent us to Marsh Habour, and we changed our plans about flying to the southern islands. I started a revival that night in the church Brother Woodis attended, and Brother Vanwinkle started a meeting in another church on the island.

While we were in Marsh Harbour we char-
tered a boat, complete with crew, and went from
island to island to preach in the open air.

When we docked at an island, Mrs. Arnold,
Brother VanWinkle, and I went ashore and visited every house within walking distance and invited the people to come to the service we were
going to hold. Then we returned to the boat and
waited. We soon learned that the people would
not come to a preaching service, even in the open
air, without dressing in their best apparel.

After about an hour the people would start
arriving, and soon we would have a good crowd.
We led the people in singing, then preached and
gave an invitation for the lost to trust Jesus as
Saviour. Then we moved on to the next island
and had another service.

That day of visiting the various islands and
preaching from the boat is one of my choice
memories of mission work in the Bahamas.

The people dressing for the open-air services
reminds me of how they always dressed for religious services. There is the memory of the dedication of the church at West End that I and some
men of my church helped to build. It was not a
simple dedication services. The people had a flare
for drama, and they dressed for the occasion.

The women all dressed in white, and the men
all dressed in black. They first met in the lodge

hall where they had been having services. There they went through an elaborate ceremony of song and testimony to close the old temple. Then they marched to the new church, singing as they went.

When they arrived at the church the door was locked, and they stood outside and had a ceremony. They finished by singing a song entitled, *Open Up the Temple.* Then the doors of the church were flung open, and the people went inside for an elaborate dedication service. Even the governor of the island attended the service.

Another occasion for the people to dress in their best was a baptizing. Again the men dressed in black and the women in white. They went to the church, then marched to the coast and formed two rows facing the sea. In the front of the rows one person held a Christian flag, and another held a Bahamian flag.

The pastor waded out in the water and waited while the converts walked between the rows of people to the edge of the water. Then he came for the converts, one at a time, led them out in the water and baptized them. Each time the pastor baptized a convert the two people with the flags dipped them as the convert went under the water and raised them as the candidate came out of the water.

After the end of the two weeks of revivals at Marsh Harbour we took off in beautiful weather to fly home, and I cleared the field and turned toward Florida. We flew down the chain of islands, and soon Grand Bahama came into view.

I thought of landing and refueling, but I reasoned that we would lose time, and it was possible that they would not have the kind of gasoline my plane required. I checked my gas gauges and saw that I had plenty of gas to make landfall in Florida, so I flew on.

We flew down the length of Grand Bahama and started the flight over open water. Grand Bahama faded in the distance. and for a short time we were out of sight of land. Then the Florida coast came into view. I relaxed and radioed the tower at West Palm Beach for permission to land. We landed there, refueled, and took off for the flight to Lexington.

I am thankful to this day that God stopped me from flying to the southern islands as I had planned. That would have been an extremely dangerous flight. I could easily have missed one of the tiny islands where I planned to land and refuel. I could have run out of fuel and had to ditch in the ocean. If that had happened it is likely that we would never have been found, and I would not be writing this book. I am thankful that our God is a God of miracles and that He has taken care of me through all the years that I have served Him.

Chapter 22

Foreign Travel Miracles

Deliverance From a Barbwire Prison

In 1954, for more than three weeks, Dr. B. R. Lakin, Dr. Dallas Billington, and I, along with some 20 others, traveled in the Holy Land. That was just six years after the founding of the State of Israel. Jerusalem was a divided city, having Israeli and Arab sectors, and tensions were high throughout the region.

Early one morning several of our party left Jerusalem to go to the rock-red city of Petra. We were driven to the airport in limousines and boarded a plane for Ma'An, Jordan. The usual route from Jerusalem to Petra was to fly to Ammon, Jordan, then travel the rest of the way by automobile, but for some reason our plane was not to fly to Ammon but to Ma'An, a small town in the desert, not far from Petra.

Our plane passed over mountains, valleys and, flat, sandy desert waste before it reached Ma'An.

When we landed in Ma'An, an inordinate amount of time passed before they opened the door of the plane for us to deplane. When they finally opened it, we were allowed to walk down some portable stairs into a circle of menacing armed guards.

The guards put our entire party under arrest, loaded us in automobiles, drove us some miles over a desert road, and stopped in a barbed wire enclosure.

Dr. Billington and I rode in the car with Emil, our Christian Arab guide. I was glad for that because Emil knew the language and could talk with our driver and try to find out why we were under arrest. And talk, he did! He was angry, and it appeared that he told the driver exactly what he thought of the situation.

Fifteen or more of our traveling companions were in the other cars. Included in that number was my longtime friend, Dr. B. R. Lakin. Knowing him as I did, I knew that he was extremely worried.

Our guide finally told us that we were being held on the pretense that we were traveling without passports. The hotel in Jerusalem had taken our passports when we checked in, and they would not return them until we checked out. That was standard practice, and our captors knew that perfectly well. They also knew that we had crossed no borders. We had left Jerusalem, Jordan that morning, and we were still in Jordan. They knew also that we were to return to the hotel that night. Our captors did not have a valid charge, but that did not keep them from taking us captive.

Dr. Dallas Billington and I sat in the car that had transported us from the airport and looked out at the armed men who were guarding us. Beyond them were swirls of barbwire that enclosed our makeshift prison. There were more guards at the gate. We could not imagine what would happen next.

After a time our guide was allowed to leave the car to go and talk with someone. When he returned he told us that they were going to release our car so he could go to the home of the mayor of the city and confer with him.

Our driver drove out of the barbwire enclosure and along several winding streets. After traveling about ten miles he stopped the car beside a large house, and our guide got out and went in. The driver stayed in the car with Dr. Billington and I, and we could do nothing but wait and pray. I am sure that the members of our party who were still in the barbwire prison were praying also.

That was an especially bad day for me. I had been sick with an infection travelers often get in that part of the world. I had spent a day and two nights in bed in Jerusalem and I was still far from well.

After about a half hour, Emil returned to the car. "The mayor wants you to come in and partake of his hospitality," he told us.

We got out of the car and went to the door of the mayor's house. A servant invited us in and told us to be seated. Soon a maid came with coffee and some cookies. The coffee was black and strong, as it always is in that part of the world. It looked thick enough to be eaten with a spoon.

I am not a coffee drinker. I was sure the strong coffee would make me worse, but I feared that if I did not drink it my friends would never get out of the barbwire prison. I decided to make the supreme sacrifice and drank the thick, strong, coffee—every drop of it. Either the Lord helped me or the coffee had a medicinal effect. My stomach stopped hurting at once, and it did not bother me again on the trip.

After we had partaken of the mayor's hospitality, we returned to the car and were driven back to where our friends were waiting. After we returned the guards released all of us and we were allowed to continue on our way.

In that part of the world they often take prisoners for no reason. They often hold them indefinitely, and sometimes they behead them. I have no doubt that God caused our captors to let us go unharmed. That was another of God's miracles.

We spent the rest of the day exploring Petra, and in spite of what we had been through it was one of the greatest days of our tour. Our trip back to Jerusalem was uneventful, but what we went through that day will always remain high on the list of the unforgettable experiences. God performs miracles when they are needed.

Trial in Egypt

In 1977 I took a tour group to Bible lands. Egypt was one of the countries we visited, and there we had an unexpected trial. Our visit to Egypt was at the end of our tour. There was trouble in that part of the world at that time, but that is not unusual.

When our plane reached Cairo it was kept in the air so long I was beginning to wonder if it would run out of fuel. When our plane finally landed and we got off we were given an unusual reception. Each member of our party was handed a large, white pill and a glass of water and told to swallow the pill. I had no idea what the pill was for or what it would do to us. I could not warn the others not to take the pill, but I had no intention of taking it. I managed to dispose of it and to pour some of the water on the floor without being seen.

Someone who spoke English told us that they were going to take us all to the hospital in Cairo to be tested for cholera.

I told him that we were American citizens and that in no way were we going to the hospital. I also told him that I wanted to phone the American Embassy.

About that time a young doctor who had trained in America came up to me and said, "Don't let them take your people to the hospital. They are not sick now, but they will be if they go there. That hospital is filthy, and there are all kinds of germs in it."

While I was trying to reach the American Embassy on the phone, they put our people in a large room to wait.

I had to pay for every phone call, even though it was a local call. They would not accept American money, so I had to go to a bank that was in the terminal and get some of their money. I finally found the bank and they gave me a handful of their money in exchange for some of our money.

I went back to the phone and placed some of their money on the counter. The operator took some of it and supposedly placed the call. It did not go through, and I had to pay again for her to try again, and again, and again. I used up all the money the bank had given me and had to go back and get more.

When I finally reached the embassy it was past closing time. They would not come to help us, but someone agreed to talk on the phone with the man who was trying to take our party to the hospital. While talking to the man at the embassy the man agreed that we would not have to go to the hospital.

He hung up the phone and turned to me. "Your party will have to spend the night in the hotel on the third floor above the airport," he said.

That was better than going to the hospital, so I agreed. I paid for rooms in their so-called hotel for the members of our party, then went to the room where they were waiting and told them that we would have to spend the night in the hotel upstairs.

Collecting the bags for the party was not too difficult, but getting them upstairs proved to be quite a chore. The elevator was small, and it did not work properly. It would only start part of the time. When it did, it often stopped halfway up. When we finally reached the floor with a load of bags, the elevator often stopped halfway on the way back down to get another load.

We finally got all the people and all the bags to the second floor, but getting to the rooms was an ordeal. At one place in the hall a waterpipe was broken and water was pouring down upon us. When we reached the rooms we found that they left much to be desired. They were not clean, and some of them only contained a single cot for two people.

After we got our bags to our rooms we were told that they had prepared dinner for us, and it would be served on the second floor.

We went down to the second floor on the balky elevator, and sure enough they had prepared a good meal for us. We all sat down, and I offered thanks. I was thankful that at least we would not have to go to the hospital.

Just as I started to eat, a slinky looking man came out of the shadows and told me that as soon as we finished eating they were going to take all of us to the hospital. There was nothing for me to do but leave the table and go back to the phone.

No one answered at the embassy, and I assumed that it was closed for the night. I called my travel agent in America and told him what had happened. He told me to stay by the phone while he made some calls. He would get back to me. I spent the rest of the night by the phone.

I talked with the agent several times during the night, and finally, in the early morning, he called to tell me that he had scheduled a flight out of Cairo for our party at ten o'clock that morning.

I breathed a sigh of relief, but our ordeal was not over. The local guide for our party had taken our passports when we arrived. That was standard practice, but, now that we were scheduled to leave, I could not find him or reach him by phone.

The ten o'clock flight came and left without us. I went back to the phone and called our agent in America. After several calls back and forth he told me that he had scheduled a later flight for us. Our local guide did not show up with our passports until we were waiting at the gate to board the later flight.

When our flight left Egyptian air space, I realized that it was a miracle that God brought us safely through that trial.

After our ordeal was over, and we were safe at home, we learned that the government in Egypt had intended to take our party to tents they had set up in the desert and put us in quarantine. For some reason they had planned to make holding our party an international incident. To this day I remain thankful that God performed a miracle and brought us through that ordeal.

Chapter 23

Miracles in the Making

Mrs. Arnold and I flew to West Berlin August 28, 1961, so I could preach to the refugees who were escaping from Communist East Berlin. August 13 the Russians had started building a wall through the city of Berlin to keep the people in East Berlin from having contact with the people in West Berlin. At once people in East Berlin started crashing through barriers, jumping from second and third story windows, and swimming the canal to escape to the West. Many were losing their lives in their attempt to escape.

While we were in West Berlin I was busy preaching every day, and at night I could hardly sleep because God was impressing me to start another church in Lexington when we returned home.

That did not seem reasonable to me. I had

already started three churches in Lexington, but the impression grew stronger, and God gave me a vision of what the new church was to become. It was to become a great church, and in time it was to have a day school, a college, and other far-reaching ministries.

Mrs. Arnold and I returned home from West Berlin on September 11, and two weeks later we had a prayer meeting in our home. Some 30 people attended, and I took that as a confirmation that God wanted me to start another church.

The next week I started looking for a place to start a mission, but I did not find a location until the next February when I learned that the Fraternal Order of Police had a hall on Walnut Street that could be rented on Sunday mornings. I rented the hall that week and announced that I was going to start preaching there. A number of people came to the first service, and I told them that I was going to have Sunday school and preaching services there every Sunday.

Attendance grew from the beginning, and on Thanksgiving Night, the following November, we organized a church with 100 charter members.

The next January we found a house and 6 acres of land for sale on Clays Mill Road for 35 thousand dollars. The price was reasonable, even then, but we only had 100 dollars in our building fund, and I knew it would be a step of faith to buy it.

I thought we would be able to borrow a thousand dollars from the bank, and I asked the real estate agent if the people who owned the property would take a thousand dollars down and let us make monthly payments on the balance.

He was sure they would not sell the property on consignment with only a thousand dollars down, but he thought they might sell it if we would pay 3 thousand down. I thought the church might be able to borrow the 3 thousand, so I agreed to offer that much down.

The next day the agent called and told me the owner had agreed to take my offer. Elated, I went to the bank to ask for a 3 thousand dollar loan. I gave the loan officer the information he required, but, to my dismay, he refused to make the loan. His reason was that we did not have enough property owners in our membership to sign the note.

Disappointed, I went away and prayed for the Lord to tell me what to do. At once a plan came to my mind, and I returned to the bank.

"Will you loan 30 of my members 1 hundred dollars each?" I asked the loan officer. "If you will issue monthly payment books to them, I will send the 30 people in to sign the notes. I will keep the books, collect the money, and make payments to the bank."

"I never heard of a plan like that, but it will

work," he said.

We got the money we needed and closed the deal on the property on January 24. The house on the property was rented, and the occupant had a lease and was not willing to move until it expired at the end of May.

By February the FOP Hall had became too small for our congregation, so we moved our services to Kenwick School on Henry Clay Boulevard and worshiped there until the end of May.

The first of June we put up a tent on our property and started having services in it. We knew that we could not stay in the tent after the weather started getting cold, but we could not start building until we paid our loan to the bank so we could refinance and get a construction loan on our property.

At prayer meeting one Wednesday night, not long after we moved into the tent, the Lord told me to tell the people that we were to pay off the loan to the bank in the next three weeks. One of the men of the church almost had a nervous breakdown. He was sure the church was going broke, and that the members would go broke as well.

When I went to the post office one morning the next week, I got a thick letter in the mail. I opened it and it contained 16 one hundred dollar bills. An unsigned note in the letter said that we were to use the money on the church loan. That was not enough to pay the loan, but it was a good start.

The next Sunday I took great pleasure in counting the 16 hundred dollar bills into the hand of the doubting brother in front of the congregation.

We raised the rest of the money that was needed, paid our loan to the bank, got a clear deed, refinanced, and started building our first auditorium.

We worked almost night and day to get the new building far enough along so we could have services in it before cold weather. We started having services in the unfinished building in mid-October.

We continued to work on the building through the winter, and the congregation continued to grow. When we dedicated the auditorium on May 3, 1964, we had 275 members.

The church continued to grow, and we broke ground for a two-story educational building in September, 1966. In November of that year all previous records were broken. The membership was more than 300, and the Sunday school attendance reached 285 on a high Sunday.

In time we had the educational building almost finished and the parking area blacktopped. We had a bus ministry, and the church was continuing to grow. I wanted to spend the rest of my life pastoring the church, but the Lord was leading me to go into evangelism. My call and my work as an evangelist is covered in the next chapter.

It was not God's will for me to finish the vision He had given me of what the church was to become. I was to leave that task to others. I did not question God's leading, and I never looked back

Three pastors, Eugene Holmes, Rex McPherson, and Mike Carruthers served the church between the time I resigned in 1972 and the call of Dr. Jeff Fugate in 1991.

God's Ways Are Marvelous

One day early in 1979, while in my car in Nicholasville, I tuned in WSGS, a powerful radio station in Hazard, Kentucky. It was coming in like a local station. I had been looking for a station to put *The Voice of the Appalachians* broadcast on that would cover much of East Kentucky, and I realized that I had found it.

A short time later I arranged to go on the station, and a truck driver I had never met volunteered to pay the cost of the broadcast until listeners started supporting it.

The program was on the air at 10:00 o'clock on Sunday Nights, and Pastor Sam Fugate, founder and pastor of Bible Baptist Church in Hazard, and his family became regular listeners. Jeff Fugate was then a boy of 15.

Later that year, Brother Sam invited me to hold a revival for him in his church. I became friends with him and his family, and I was greatly impressed with Jeff. He was already active in the Lord's work, but I never dreamed that one day he would become pastor of the church I had founded in Lexington. Even then God was grooming him for the work he is now doing. God put that all together.

The vision I had while I was in Germany continues, with God performing miracle after miracle through the ministry of Dr. Jeff Fugate and Clays Mill Road Baptist Church.

Dr. Fugate's pastorate at Clays Mill has been and continues to be phenomenal. He has led the church in an aggressive program of soul winning and church building, and he has started other far-reaching ministries. He can best tell of the blessings of God on his ministry in his own words.

In May of 1991 I became the fifth pastor of Clays Mill Road Baptist Church. The church had been founded by my good friend, Dr. Louis Arnold. The church had gone down in attendance, and there were only 18 people present in my first service on a Wednesday night. There was about 35 in attendance at my first Sunday morning service.

The church had started a Christian School in the 70s, and it was one of the schools that took a strong stand for Christian education, leading to the State Supreme Court ruling in favor of Christian education in 1980.

After I became pastor we spent the first few weeks painting, cleaning, and working on the building to get it ready for the great things I believed God was going to do.

In the month of June, 1991, Evangelist Joe Boyd held a revival meeting for us. We went soul winning every day during the meeting, and by the end of the week we had seen many converts come to Christ, with 63 people following the Lord in believers baptism.

In the early days of my pastorate at Clays Mill Road Baptist Church, I often visited my good friend, Dr. Louis Arnold, at his office in Nicholasville. He always took time to visit with me, to counsel me, to answer my questions, and to give me guidance. He encouraged me to stay by the stuff, to keep on winning souls, to keep on preaching the Word of God, and singing the old-time hymns and Gospel songs that we Baptists have enjoyed through the years.

The old-time way is still working. We now have over 400 people who are active each week in winning souls!

We have had an average growth of 100 per year since I became pastor 17 years ago. This year our attendance has continued to grow. This spring (2008) we averaged 1,700 each Sunday. This fall we started having multiple services to accommodate the crowds.

In 1998 I began holding tent revivals in our state and across the nation because of my burden for revival. I often preached 100 nights straight in June, July, and August.

Good crowds attended our tent meetings, and people were saved. During these meetings I became burdened to start new churches that would go out and win souls, run bus routes, and actively work to make a difference for the cause of Christ in their towns.

As I began to look for men as candidates to start these churches I learned of another need, the need to train young men and prepare them for the ministry. That was when I became burdened to start Commonwealth Baptist College.

In 1999 we began teaching classes in preparation and organization of a Bible College. In 2003, after three years of praying and a financial miracle, we purchased a 25 acre campus on Versailles Road where our college is housed to-day. We now have 130 students from 26 states and excitement is growing about what God is doing at Commonwealth Baptist College.

Currently we are preparing to start our 20th new church! Of the churches we have started, 17 are in Kentucky. I have a goal to see 50 soul winning churches started in the state.

The 17 churches we have already started are having an influence in the state, such as stopping casino gambling in our state. While there were many people involved in the opposition of the expanded gambling, we did lead the way!

In the past Dr. Arnold influenced my father, the church he pastored, and my-self by way of the radio program he conducted. I have been on radio all of the years that I have been the pastor of

Clays Mill Road Baptist Church. Since September of 1995, 1 have had the privilege to be the speaker on "The Voice of the Appalachians broadcast." This radio network was started by Dr. B. R. Lakin. After 6 years he turned the broadcast over to Dr. Arnold. He was the speaker on the "Voice" for 21 years before he turned it over to me.

Today the broadcast is heard on more than 40 radio stations in several states. We have a daily response from the ministry of radio.

In 2005 the Lord allowed us to purchase 117 acres of land in Garrard County to start the Circle C Baptist Ranch. Of all places, it is near Dr. Arnold's birthplace in Buckeye, Kentucky.

We have already built 8 hand-crafted log cabins and a beautiful cafeteria which will allow us to have not only camp in the summer but retreats through the fall. In the 3rd year of our summer camp we had over 1,000 campers in attendance.

In 2002 1 became the editor of the Church Bus News that was founded by the late Dr. Wally Beebe. This is a nationwide publication that is distributed to encourage and instruct bus ministries across the nation.

Our church is now the host site for the National Bus Convention held each year in October. In 2007 we had delegates to attend from 26 of the 50 states. Along with the Church Bus News we operate Beebe Publications which provides materials for every area of church work to churches all across America.

One of the slogans we use is, "We are just getting started" and I believe it! While the Lord has done marvelous things for us and we have seen thousands of people come to Christ, there is great excitement and anticipation of what God is going to do in the future.

Dr. Fugate did not mention that he held a Patriotic Rally at Applebee's Ball Park in Lexington on July 4, 2002 with an attendance of 6300. Nor did he mention that Clays Mill Road Baptist Church has a thriving Spanish ministry that was started in 2001.

Clays Mill Road is the fastest growing church in Lexington, and one of the fastest growing in the state of Kentucky. The present Sunday attendance is an average of about 1600 with a high day of 2300. The ministry of Clays Mill Road Baptist Church is truly a miracle.

Chapter 24

An Evangelist at Last

From the day I entered the ministry I knew I was called to be an evangelist, but an older preacher told me that I ought to serve as a pastor for a time before entering the field of evangelism. "You will gain experience, and you will learn how to be a help to a pastor," he told me.

I took his advice and became a pastor, and I stayed in the pastorate longer than I had planned. I enjoyed the pastorate. I loved my people, and I found that it was not easy to leave them. Besides, though the salary I received as a pastor was small, it did provide a regular income. As an evangelist I knew that I would have no certain income, that I would have to live by faith, and that I would have to be gone from home much of the time. But I knew God wanted me to be an evangelist, and during the years I served as a pastor, I also held every revival meeting possible.

During those years I was gaining valuable experience, and the Lord was preparing me for the work I was to do later in life.

In those years I went to hear every well-known evangelist who held meetings within driving distance of where I lived. I listened to them preach and watched them in action. I learned all I could from them, and their fires lighted my torch and helped to keep it burning.

The first books that fell into my hands after I started preaching were two small paperback books of sermons by D. L. Moody, and I read them over and over. Other books of his sermons were then on sale by Moody Press for 25 cents per copy. Quarters were hard to come by in those days, but every time I got a quarter I could spare I ordered another book of Moody's sermons.

Later I read books by other men. A book by L. R. Scarbough, entitled, *With Christ After the Lost,* fired my soul. From that book, I learned much about winning people to Christ. R. A. Torrey's great book on the Holy Spirit showed me my need of God's anointing power, and it caused me to search the Scriptures to learn more about the Holy Spirit and how He works through men. It drove me to my knees to pray for the power of God upon my ministry.

Later, a preacher friend told me about a set

of twenty volumes of sermons by T. De Witt
Talmage. Somehow I managed to scrape together
the money to buy a used set of his books. Talmage
preached on all kinds of subjects. Some of his
sermons did nothing for me, but others were mas-
terpieces. He was a master sermon builder, and
he was eloquent beyond description. From his
books I learned much about how to prepare sermons.

I read books by other men, most of them great
preachers of bygone days. Especially I read sermons by evangelists who had been greatly used
of God. Through those years of studying and
praying, I knew I was preparing for the day when
I would become an evangelist.

Finally the day came when I began to pray
definitely about going into evangelism. Not long
after that, I was on the campus of Tennessee
Temple University, in Chattanooga, Tennessee,
along with many other pastors from across
America. Services were being held in the High-
land Park Baptist Church, and during the morning sessions, Dr. Lee Roberson conducted his
daily radio broadcast from the platform. One
morning while the broadcast was in progress, to
my surprise, Dr. Roberson called me to the platform and proceeded to interview me. It really
threw me when he asked, "When are you going

into evangelism full time?"

I had told no one that I was wrestling with that very question, so he had no way of knowing that I had been praying about that decision for weeks.

"I—I really don't know," I stammered.

Dr. Roberson then told me that I ought to go into evangelism and stay there for the rest of my life. "That is where you belong," he said.

Soon after that I became convinced that the Lord wanted me to resign the church I had organized and built and step out into evangelism full time. I had no assurance that I would be invited to hold meetings, and I had no guarantee of an income, but I believed that the Lord would take care of me.

One Sunday morning not long after that, when I entered the auditorium of my church, I heard from Heaven. The Lord could not have spoken more clearly if He had sent me a telegram. The Lord told me that He wanted me to resign my church that day, and I did not question His leading. That morning, at the close of the service, I called the men of the church together and told them that I was going to resign. I told them that I did not have my letter of resignation written, but I would write it that afternoon, and I read it to the church that night.

Thirty days later, I preached my farewell sermon and told the people good-bye. I was out of a job. I no longer had a salary, and I had to depend on the Lord to open doors for me and to meet my needs.

July the first, 1972, I stepped out by faith and became a full-time evangelist. That day I made a covenant with the Lord that I would not make any effort to get meetings but would trust Him to open doors for me. Immediately doors began to open, and soon I was holding meetings in several states each year. I have now been in evangelism for thirty-six years, and the Lord continues to open doors for me.

In my years as an evangelist I have held city-wide meetings, preached in Bible conferences and camp meetings, and held church revivals from Florida to California, and from Mississippi to Massachusetts.

I have missed pastoring. I have missed people who had become dear to me, but I have never regretted becoming an evangelist.

In meetings I have held, I have seen the lost converted, backsliders reclaimed, Christians revitalized, and churches set aflame. Pastors often tell me that their churches experience healthy growth following my meetings, and many of them have invited me to hold meetings in their churches again and again.

After I had been in evangelism for a few years, a strong church with great potential wanted me to be their pastor. I wanted to take that church. My wife wanted me to take it, but I waited and prayed for the Lord's leading. When the answer came, I knew that God wanted me to stay in evangelism. That settled it. I told the men of the church that, much as I would like to be their pastor, the Lord had told me to stay in evangelism. Enough time has now passed for me to look back and see that God's way was the best way.

For one thing, if I had become pastor of that church, with its varied ministries, I would not have had time to write the books the Lord has led me to write. The pressures of evangelism are great, but I am able to make time to write, and writing has become a large part of my ministry.

At age 94 I remain active in the ministry. I continue to conduct a daily radio broadcast. I travel and preach almost every Sunday, and I often preach during the week. Also, I often preach to preachers in camp meetings and fellowship meetings. That is one of the highlights of my present ministry. I enjoy the fellowship with the preachers, and I enjoy the privilege of preaching to them.

I publish *The Arnold Report* every month,and I continue to write a book each year. My writing is reaching people I will never see in this world. The books I have written, and others I plan to write, will be in the world long after I have gone to my reward. They are and will be an extension of my ministry.

Chapter 25

Writing Goes on the Front Burner

My mother had a gift for writing, and I think she may have prayed that I would be a writer as well. If in Heaven she knows about the books I have written, I think she must be pleased.

From the time I started preaching I felt that the Lord wanted me to be a writer as well as a preacher, but there came a time when my call to write was as definite as my call to preach. I answered the call at once, for I had been attempting to write long before the call came.

From childhood I had tried to write. I used to make up stories and compose poems as I walked the mile to and from my house to school. Walking seemed to stimulate my mind and often started me composing a story or a poem. I often put my thoughts on paper when I got to where I was going. One of the things I wrote on those daily walks was a poem entitled *The Schoolhouse in the Wood.*

I composed *The Schoolhouse in the Wood* and committed it to memory as I walked to and from Westpoint, the two-room school I attended.

Later I wrote the poem on paper and took it to the editor of The Central Record, our county paper in Lancaster, Kentucky. That poem, was the first thing I ever had published, and I was greatly pleased when I saw it in the paper. I am printing the poem here with some appropriate comments.

The Schoolhouse in the Wood

Between the crossroads once there stood,
  A one-roomed structure, plain and drear.
It was the schoolhouse in the wood,
  With mountains towering in the rear.
To grace the eyes, the wild rose grew
  Upon the mountain's jagged side,
And across a sky of blue,
  Like a golden ball the sun did ride.

Part of the preceding verse was based on my imagination. The school I attended was not in the woods, and there were no mountains in the rear. At the time I wrote this poem, I had never seen a mountain.

The next four verses of the poem were based on my experience as a student in the country school I attended. Young as I was, I had a memory for details.

Inside the room since sharp at eight,
   The classes had gone forward slow,
For impatient students scarce could wait
   For recess so they could go.
While waiting thus, they whispered some,
   And sometimes paper wads did throw,
And wish that soon the hour would come
   When they could march out row by row.

Some students to their books gave heed,
   As they were thus inclined.
But some would just pretend to read,
   While wondered far afield their mind.
Some made marks upon the wall,
   And some carved initials in their desks,
For the master could not watch them all,
   Though he did his very best.

Yet oft' the cruel lash would fall,
   When some transgressor had been found,
A warning and example to them all,
   That made them quietly settle down.
The minutes lengthened into hours;
   The sun was in the western sky.
The lengthening shadows formed like
      towers,
   Reminding one of ages long gone by.

Then came the closing hour of school,
  And the students, standing row by row,
According to the master's rule
  Marched outside with footsteps slow.
Then turned upon the homeward road,
  With joyful shouts and happy play,
Sought each his home, a meek abode,
  In the cool of the dying day.

The next verse was taken partly from what I
had seen and partly from my imagination

The sky fast changed from blue to red.
  The shadows fell below.
A familiar sound was heard o'er head,
  The lonely "caw" of a lonely crow.
A smoldering fire, the sun's rim glowed,
  Through whispering pines on the
    mountain's crest.
And dazzling, changing colors flowed
  Across the sky from the golden west.

From this point on the poem is written purely
from my imagination.

In the dying splendor, hand in hand,
  Two loitered on their way,
Enjoyed the fragrance of God's land,
  The closing of God's day.
A boy and girl, behind the rest,
  With spirits running high
With emotions they could not express,
  Forgot that night was drawing nigh.

'Twas Mary Allen, a maiden sweet,
  Just blooming into womanhood,
A graceful creature from head to feet,
  The tranquil beauty of the wood.
Like golden rod, her wavy hair.
  Her eyes were violet blue.
Her cheeks like roses, rich and rare,
  Her smile was winning, true.

And David Long, a slender lad,
  With eyes as blue as steel,
Loved Mary Allen, the only girl he'd had.
  And as they walked across the field,
He asked her if she would be his wife,
  When they were come of age.
She smiled and said, "I'll share your life,
  Until we reach the final page."

Now years have past; they have grown
  old.
  Together they have shared the years.
They've known the heat and the cold,
  The sunshine and the tears.
And now beside a new schoolhouse,
  They watch their grandchildren play,
And smiling through their tears rejoice
  That they have reached this day.

I now see the shortcomings of this poem I

wrote as a child, and I consider it most kind that the editor printed it in our local newspaper.

Many of the things I wrote in those early days have been lost. Perhaps it is best that they were, but I am glad this poem survived.

I was ill prepared for the task when God called me to write, but I started writing anyway. My early writing was a kind of on the job training, and much of what I wrote ended up in the trash can. That was where it belonged.

In time I started submitting some articles and poems to magazines. Many of them brought only rejection slips. They named them right, and that is exactly how I felt, rejected. But I kept on writing, and finally one day a magazine accepted something I had written. They paid me for it too—a whole dollar. That was the most appreciated dollar I ever earned. It meant that at last I was a paid, published author.

After that more and more of the things I wrote were accepted and paid for. In time some of what I wrote appeared in leading religious publications. I really felt that I had arrived when something I wrote was published in a magazine that went into 104 countries of the world.

I finished writing my first inspirational novel, *The Legend of Old Faithful,* just before the outbreak of World War II. A lady who belonged to the church I was pastoring typed it for me, and I sent it off to a publisher. At that time I had no idea that the manuscript needed to go through several revisions and be proofread several times before it was ready to submit to a publisher.

I was greatly elated when someone from the publishing company wrote and told me that they were interested in the manuscript I had submitted. (I now marvel that they were interested at all.) They wanted to submit the manuscript to another publisher they were working with, and, with my permission, they sent it off to them.

There followed anxious days of waiting. Then, to my great disappointment, I received a rejection letter. World War II had started, and because of the resulting shortage of materials and manpower, they had decided not to undertake publishing my book.

Great as that disappointment was, I have lived to thank God for their decision. *The Legend of Old Faithful* was not then ready for publication. Years later, after many revisions and rewrites, it was published. Had it been published in the beginning, it would not have been as good a book as it was when it finally went to press.

For many years, because of the pressures of a busy ministry, my writing was put on the back burner. Finally, in 1983, I decided that if I was ever going to write the books I believed the Lord wanted me to write, I had better begin writing in earnest. Soon after that, some friends made it possible for me to buy a computer. I taught myself to use it and started using it to write. Since then, I have missed very few days writing,

Two years later I had a book on prophecy, *Israeli Countdown to Eternity*, published. One year after that my first novel, *The Legend of Old Faithful*, was published.

The books I have written since then have been far better received by the reading public than I ever expected. They have gone into every state and into several foreign countries. From the time *The Legend of Old Faithful* was released until the present, letters have come from thousands of readers, praising my books and urging me to keep on writing. Each year more and more people order the book I am working on as soon as I announce the title. For several years I have been numbering and autographing books that are ordered before publication, and each year the number of people who order before publication increases.

Another surprise has been that my books sell themselves. For example, someone will borrow one of my books or get one from a library. After reading it, they write to me or to one of my publishers, asking for lists of other books I have written so they can order them. I will be forever grateful to my loyal readers for making my writing ministry so successful, and, just as they have requested, I plan to keep on writing.

I have several books in my mind that I plan to write. I often think about a book for months or years before I start writing it. It is not unusual for me to have four or more books started, but I concentrate on one of them until it is finished.

I plan to keep on writing as long as the Lord gives me the health and the ability to do so.

Chapter 26
Miracles of Supply
Emergency Transportation

This is an account of how God provided needed transportation in an emergency on a never-to-be forgotten trip to a mission field.

In 1952 I flew a commercial airline to the beautiful country of Guatemala to visit and work with missionaries Robert and Trudy Neighbour and James and Taffie Humes. The plane I boarded in Miami stopped briefly in Mexico City, then took off for Guatemala. On the way we flew over beautiful mountains, wooded valleys and country that was stark, rugged, and rock covered. At length my plane landed in Guatemala City, and I got off with a movie camera and a broadcast quality, reel to reel tape recorder—one of the first ones on the market at that time.

Robert and Jim met me at the airport in a pickup truck, and we soon started on our way. I saw at once that I was in one of the most beautiful countries I had ever seen. Guatemala is called, *The Land of Eternal Spring,* and it fits the picture. It is like a flower garden with multicolored flowers blossoming everywhere. There were birds of every hue nesting and singing in the trees. Parrots, almost tame, were in the shrubs by the roadside. There are small green ones, and larger double yellowheads. In the terminal building at the airport, I had seen tame, giant macaws with bright red, yellow and blue plumage, but I had not expected to see so many parrots in the wild.

When we arrived at the mission house the Humes family had two sick babies, and by the time we finished the meetings Robert had planned for me the sick babies were worse. Both families felt that they should return to the States so the babies could receive medical care that was not available on the mission field, but they did not have enough money to pay their fares to Miami, much less all the way home. My funds were limited also.

Brother Neighbour called the airline office and asked the price of the tickets to Miami. Then we made a careful accounting of the money we all had and found that we had enough to pay for the tickets to Miami, but we would have little left when we got there. We would have to trust the Lord to get us the rest of the way home

After an overnight flight, we landed in Miami and got through customs in time for breakfast. The Neighbours had enough money for their breakfast, and I had enough to pay for breakfast for the Humes family and myself, with some left over.

While we were eating, we discussed what we should do. The Neighbours decided to stay with friends in Miami for a few days. I needed to go on to Lexington, and the Humes family needed to go to their home in Louisville, but we did not have money for the trip.

After we finished eating, we found a secluded place where we could pray. We explained our problems to the Lord, as if He did not already know. Then we returned to the waiting room and waited to see what the Lord would do.

In a few minutes, Brother Humes went off and sat down alone. A moment later a stranger sat down beside him. Then, just as if he had been asked, the stranger made a startling statement.

"You know," he said, "there's a company here that is trying to find drivers to take some cars north to their owners. They will fill the tank of one of these cars with gas and pay $10.00 in cash to anyone with a driver's license who will drive a car north and deliver it to the owner."

It did not take long for Brother Humes to re-port this to me. We investigated and found that we could indeed get a car to drive home. We decided that with the tank full of gas, $10.00 from the company, and the money I had left, we could drive the car as far as Lexington. There I could get money for the Humes family to finish the trip to Louisville and deliver the car to the owner. We would just have to go light on food on the trip.

We found our way to the company with the cars and signed the necessary papers to get one to drive home. Then they brought out an almost new car that belonged to the Governor of Illinois. They filled the tank with gas, gave us $10.00 in cash and handed us the keys.

We loaded our bags in the car and climbed in, thankful that the Lord had answered our prayers and had made it possible for us to go home in style and comfort.

Sheetrock Supplied

Soon after the end of World War II, I started a church in Lexington, Kentucky and became their pastor. Soon after that I starting building a house to live in. Because of the number of men coming home from the war and starting families, there was a shortage of houses, and that caused a building boom. New houses were going up all across the country, and building materials were in short supply. One of the lumber companies in Lexington agreed to sell me building materials, but when the time came that I needed Sheetrock they had sold out. One of the owners told me that the only Sheetrock to be had was on the black market at an exorbitant price.

I spent the rest of the day going from one lumber company to another looking for Sheetrock. None of them had any, and they had no prospect of getting any. I finally gave up, asked God to take care of the need, and went home.

The next morning I and the carpenter who was helping me were working on the house, and about midmorning a truck loaded with Sheetrock stopped out front. The driver came in and asked if I needed Sheetrock. I asked him the price, and he quoted the exact price that the lumber company would have charged me. I bought his entire load, and it was just the amount I needed.

The miracle was that the driver came to where I was building. There were new houses going up all over town. In new subdivisions, several houses were being built on a single street. I was building in an old neighborhood on a dead-end side street, and my house was the only one being built in the area. God sent the driver to where I was building just as if someone had given him directions to the location.

Money for a Broadcast

Years ago I was on several radio stations, and

I drove to some of them each day to do my broad-cast live in their studios. One of those sta-tions was in Winchester, Kentucky, about 20 miles from my office in Lexington.

One day as I started driving to Winchester to do my broadcast it seemed that the devil got in the car and rode with me. He started telling me that I was out of my mind to be broadcasting on so many radio stations. The money would not come in to pay for the radio time. I was going to go broke, and I would cause my church to go broke also.

Finally I had enough, and I said, "Devil, I did not invite you to ride with me. You get out and walk." Then I started praying.

I asked the Lord to do something to shut up the devil. I never prayed like this before, and I have never prayed like this again. I do not rec-ommend it, but on that occasion I felt that the Lord wanted me to pray as I did.

I said, "Lord, I want you to make the devil shut up. I am going to park my car at the first place that is empty on the street by the radio sta-tion. I am going to stand on the nearest street corner for five minutes by my watch. I will not speak to anybody unless they speak to me first. I want You to send me exactly enough money to pay for one broadcast on this station while I am standing there."

I found a parking place, parked the car, walked to the nearest corner, and stood there. In about two minutes a lady I did not recognize came along, recognized me and stopped.

"Brother Arnold, I want to have a part in your radio ministry." she said, and handed me some bills and some change. I thanked her, and she hurried on.

I counted the money, and it was not enough to pay for a broadcast.

"This is not enough, Lord," I prayed. "If you don't send the rest of the cost of a broadcast, the devil will always say it was an accident that I got this much." I looked at my watch and saw that I only had two minutes to go. "Lord, You have to hurry. Time is running out," I said.

Just then a man I did not recognize came by walking fast. He handed me some money and hurried on. To make the answer to my prayer even more difficult, this radio station charged an odd amount for a fifteen minute broadcast. There had to be some change involved to have enough to pay for a broadcast. I counted the money I had in my hand, and it was the exact amount I needed to the penny. I said, "Shut up, devil," I said. "God is real, and He is taking care of me."

Daily Bread Supplied

The account of how God supplied daily bread for me and Dr. Mordicia Ham is given in my book, *Great Preachers I have Known.* That day I had no money to pay for our meal, and it was truly a miracle the way God sent the money to pay for it at the last minute.

Miracle Contact in Germany

The account of another outstanding miracle is also given in *Great Preachers I have Known.* In it I tell how God arranged my contact to preach to the refugees during the time when Russia was building the Berlin Wall. I flew to West Berlin without knowing a word of German and with only the name of one contact that I was told I would not be able to reach.

It was a miracle how the contact and I were brought together after a soldier's German wife made only two phone calls.

Miracle of Training

A Miracle of training is covered in detail in the chapter on Dr. Frank Norris *in Great Preachers I have Known.*

Chapter 27

Unforgettable Events

Horse Ride at Night

When I arose at my home in Ashland, Kentucky on a beautiful spring morning, years ago, I had no way of knowing that when night came I would find myself riding a huge workhorse, still wearing his harness, through a dark woods in the rain. Nor could I know that the silent stranger riding beside me would make a startling, and potentially dangerous revelation before the journey ended.

Early that morning I left home, picked up some preachers, and started to South Central Kentucky to participate in an area-wide revival. We drove to Lancaster and stopped at the home of Pastor Roy Gabbard, the coordinator of the meetings.

Brother Gabbard gave us a warm reception, and we sat down and talked for awhile. Then he turned to me and said, "Brother Arnold, since you have the car, I suggest that you drop this man in the first town and the next man in the next town and the next man in the next town, and so on. You take the last church down the road."

I realized that not only was I being sent to the last place down the road, but most likely it would be the place with the least opportunity.

By the time I delivered the preachers to the towns where they were to preach, the sky had become overcast, and it looked as if it were going to rain. With some trepidation I drove to the next town. Then, following the directions Brother Gabbard had given me, I turned onto a gravel road, and followed it for a few miles, watching for a dirt lane that turned off to the right.

When I found the lane, I discovered that recent rains had turned it into a rutted, mud lane. With a sinking heart, I turned on the lane and started driving along it. In one place a small wooden culvert that had been built over a stream had slipped out of the road, and I had to get out and put it back in the road before I could go on. That is the only time I ever had to put a bridge across a stream before continuing a journey.

The mud lane meandered across a field and through a deep woods. At last I came out of the woods and found a house, the only one I had seen since leaving the gravel road. I stopped my car, got out, went to the door, and rapped. Shortly, a man opened the door and looked at me over the top of his glasses.

"I am the preacher," I greeted.

"What preacher?" he asked, looking puzzled.

"I came to hold a revival. Aren't you people expecting a revival?"

"Not as I know anything about," he replied.

"Thank you," I said. "I'll be on my way."

"No," he countered. "Since you're here, you might as well stay. While the old woman is gettin' supper, I'll send the kids around to tell the neighbors that we're going to have a service."

"Is there is a church nearby?" I questioned.

"Yeah, we got a church."

Just then it started drizzling rain. I knew the rain would make the muddy lane even worse than it was already, and I started wondering how I would get my car back to the road. About that time a man rode up on a huge workhorse. He was leading another equally large workhorse. Both horses had harness on them.

"Come on in," my host invited, holding the screen door open.

"I had better get my car back to the road before the lane gets impassible," I told him.

I turned to the man on the horse. "Will you follow me out to the road with your team?" I asked. "I'll leave my car in somebody's barn lot, and I'll ride back on the horse you're leading."

He nodded that he would.

"I'll be back before long," I told the man in the doorway, as I started back to my car.

It was a good thing the man followed me with the horses, because I got stuck in the mud at least twice, and he had to pull me out. It was almost dark by the time we reached the road, and I found a place to park my car.

By the time I got the car parked, mounted the horse, and we started back, I could not see the road, but the horses knew their way. I remember well the sound of the horses' hooves on that muddy lane, and I still remember how the mud splattered on me. I could not see the man riding beside me, but from time to time I could feel him brush against me when the horses got too close together.

I attempted to engage the man in conversation, but he would not talk. He would not even answer questions I directed at him. At length I gave up, and we rode on in silence.

We soon reached the darkest part of the woods, and I could see nothing, not a star in the sky, not the silhouette of a tree, not even the shadow of the man and the big horse beside me.

I became aware of the sounds of the night,

the muffled sloshing of the horses' hooves, the clanking of the harness chains, and the croaking of small frogs in a nearby stream. Suddenly my companion broke his silence.

"I just got out of the asylum yesterday," he stated.

I could feel the hair rising on the back of my neck. Fervently I hoped they had not let him out too soon. The man said no more. Apparently he was content with that simple statement.

The rain continued to fall in a slow drizzle. I could feel the cold, wet drops pelting my face. Then a light ahead signaled the end of our journey. I breathed a sigh of relief. I would soon be out of the dark and the rain, and away from danger—if there was any.

I soon sat down to a good meal with the family that had made me welcome. After we finished eating, the family got ready to go to church. Then my host brought out an old kerosene lantern and lit it, and we stepped out into the dark, rainy night.

When we reached the church, there were no more than a dozen people present. There was no one there to play the ancient piano, so we sang a song or two without it. I attempted to preach, but no one appeared to pay any attention to what I was saying. Most of those present appeared to go to sleep, and one man played with a large, gold watch chain until the end of the service.

It was evident that they were not interested in having a revival. After the service someone told me that the church building was soon to be demolished because of a hydroelectric dam that was being built in the area. All the people were going to move away, because their houses were going to be torn down. I thanked them for coming and told them that this was the end of the meeting.

The next morning I walked out to my car and started home. Brother Gabbard had told me that he was going to hold a meeting in a country church, near a town where I had dropped one of the preachers, so I stopped to see him on my way. I was embarrassed to tell him of my failure, but he was relieved.

The night before he had preached to a large crowd. It looked as if they were going to have a good meeting, but, because of a death in his church family, he had to return home. So he wanted me to stay and take the meeting. He would preach that night before leaving for home, and he would introduce me to the people. I agreed to stay and finish the meeting for him.

There was a good crowd that night. Brother Gabbard was a good preacher, and he preached a good sermon. At the end of the service, he told the people that he was leaving and that I was going to take over the meeting. Their disappointment was evident. I was a young man at the time, and I probably did not look like much of a preacher to them.

Despite the disappointment, a good crowd came to the ten o'clock service the next morning. The power of God was upon the service from its beginning. While we were singing in the opening service, a young woman started weeping, and deep conviction settled upon the congregation. I stopped the song and called for an invitation hymn. A number of people, including the young woman, responded to the invitation at once. I did not even preach that morning. During the rest of the week, we had a blessed revival, and I made some lifelong friends.

From that experience I learned that we should never say anything is bad until God has finished with it, for He often turns failure into success.

Invaded by KKK

In 1947 I was scheduled to hold a revival in the Pleasant Hill Baptist Church, four miles from Lenoir City, Tennessee. I flew my plane to Knoxville, and Pastor G. R. Reynolds met me at the airport and drove me to where I was to stay.

Brother Emmett Griffin, a blind musician, who was a student at Tennessee Temple College (now a university), played the piano for the congregational singing and sang solos each evening. He was quite an attraction and helped to draw overflow crowds.

The meeting was better than average, but that did not make a strong impression on my memory, for the Lord was giving me better than average meetings everywhere I went. But something did happen one night during that meeting that I have never forgotten.

That night, as we were getting ready to start the service, the pastor whispered and told me that the Ku Klux Klan was coming to the service.

I had never had the Klan to attend a revival service before, so I did not know what to expect. I had heard that sometimes Klan members attended revivals, wearing their hoods and robes, but that they usually did not disturb the services. They had been known to march past the offering plates at the front of the church, with each man placing a $5.00 bill in the plate. If they did that tonight, I thought that would not be a bad idea, but I would much rather for them not to come. I did not know a great deal about the Klan, but I had heard that they were against black people, so I did not want to be involved with them. If they did come, I decided I would ignore them and preach the Gospel as usual.

When the time came to start the service, the Klan had not made an appearance. I breathed a bit easier, thinking that perhaps they would not come, but I kept looking at the seats that someone had reserved for them in the center section of the church.

About halfway through the song service there was a stir about the door, and about 20 men, wearing white robes and hoods, filed in and seated themselves in the reserved section. The people who were already in the church did not react openly, yet I could feel tension in the atmosphere.

Soon one of the hooded men arose, walked to the front of the church, interrupted the service, and made a short speech. The content of the speech must have been bland, for I remember nothing that he said. After he returned to his seat, the service continued.

When the time came for me to preach, I preached to everyone, including those in the Klan. None of the Klan members responded in any way. I thought perhaps their commitment to the Klan precluded their response to the Gospel. At any rate, I was glad that I did not belong to an organization that causes a man to hide his identity behind a robe and a hood.

Someone made a picture of the Klansmen and

gave me a copy. I still have the picture. It serves only to remind me of a meeting I held long ago. I am not interested in a hood and robe in this world. I am looking forward to a robe and a crown in the world to come.

A Funny Thing Along the Way

This is the story of a pastoral call that gave me something to chuckle about. Years ago, during my days as a pastor, I made a call in a home where the wife and the children were Christians, but the husband was an open sinner. He was involved in chicken fighting. He was not above using bad language, and he was frequently intoxicated. I had often tried to win him to Christ, but had not been successful, though he always appeared glad to see me.

He was often away from home, but one evening when I called on the family, I found him there. He had been drinking, and had imbibed enough to make him overly friendly and talkative. He monopolized the conversation, and he kept patting me on the shoulder and telling me how much he liked me.

At last I decided it was useless to try to talk to the other members of the family, so I turned to him.

"Get on your knees, my friend. I'm going to pray for you," I said. He got on his knees, and I knelt beside him and put my arm around him.

"Lord, I want to pray for this man, but of course he is drunk," I began.

"No, I'm not, Lord," he interrupted.

I suppose he thought that the Lord wouldn't notice that he was drunk, and he didn't want me to tell on him.

Chapter 28

Looking to the Future

Years ago Solomon wrote: *"Who is she that looketh forth as the morning, fair as the moon, clear as the sun, and terrible as an army with banners?" (Song of Solomon 6:10).*

Morning time is the time of planning and looking forward to the opportunities of the day. The morning time of life is also a time of planning, of dreams, and of visions. It is unfortunate that as we grow older we often lose sight of our dreams and begin to live in the past.

In our youth, our emotions were strong and our excitement was easily aroused. As a result much of what happened was indelibly stamped in memory. So memories of our past are our strongest memories, and they are the ones that stay with us through life. When we come to the place in life where nothing exciting is happening, we retain few memories of day to day events.

Since most of our recent memories are not stroug, it is natural for us to go back and relive the exciting, happy memories of the past.

That is a pleasant way to spend our time, but we should not spend so much time reminiscing that we let the remaining days of our lives pass us by with few worthwhile achievements. As we grow older, if we have health and energy, life can still be exciting, productive, and rewarding.

There is nothing wrong with recalling treasured memories of long ago, as long as we do not get stuck back there. I try not to do that. I enjoy recalling those happy days of long ago, but I keep focused on what I plan to do in the future.

I like to keep in mind the words of Paul, the Apostle. "*. . . but this one thing I do, forgetting those things which are behind, and reaching forth unto those things which are before, I press toward the mark for the prize of the high calling of God in Christ Jesus*" *(Phil. 3:13, 14).*

At the beginning of each new year, instead of making New Year's resolutions, I make a New Year's dedication and ask the Lord to help me serve Him better than I did in the preceding year. Also, I ask Him to help me accomplish more in His service than in any previous year.

I cannot relive the years that are gone. I cannot do again the things I used to do, but I can do things now that I could not have done back then. The coming days of my life will offer new opportunities and challenges, and with God's help, I want to make the most of them. I frequently pray that the Lord will make my remaining days the most productive days of my life.

I do not know how long I will live, but I do not plan to quit serving the Lord as long as I am able to walk, think, and work. I have too many things to do for me to give up before the Lord gets through with me. Even then, when my time comes, as Dr. Lakin used to say, "I'll be holding onto the willow bushes."

While I'm working at present tasks, I keep many things in mind that I want to do in the future. One of the things I plan to do is write more books. Writing books involves more time and work than I ever dreamed possible, but writing them keeps me busy and excited. And I know that my books are being used by the Lord to bless many lives.

One day my body will wear out, and I will not be able to do as much as I am presently doing. But I do not plan to hasten that day by allowing my body to rust out. I believe in keeping busy. I believe in exercising my body and keeping my muscles strong. I do several kinds of aerobic exercises, and I'm not above manual labor. I raise a garden each year, and I do repair work on our buildings. I would do more of that sort of thing if time permitted. I avoid a couch and an easy chair like the plague. I believe rocking chairs have killed more people than shovels ever have. I eat a healthful diet. I take vitamins, and sometimes minerals and herbs. I try to drink enough water, and I insist on getting enough sleep. I have learned that I function better if my body is not walking around starved for sleep.

If the time comes when I am no longer able to work, I will do all I can to keep my mind active. And I will still look to the future. There is no end of life for a Christian. We will experience a transition, but there will be no end of consciousness.

One day I will reach the end of my journey on earth. I know not whether it will be at the Coming of the Lord or at the breaking of the pitcher at the fountain or the wheel at the cistern, as Solomon puts it in Ecclesiastes 12:6.

I know that one day I will leave this world and go to a world where there are no tears and no good-byes. I have often wondered just how my transition will take place. Perhaps the Lord will come again in my lifetime, and I will be caught up with my loved ones and friends to meet Him in the air. Or it may be that I will wear my body out—that one day I will walk my last mile across the last field and pause at the bank of a river. It may be that my friends and family will walk with me to the riverbank, and I will have time to tell them good-bye. Their hands may hold my hand until the clasp is broken and I slide into the river.

For a fleeting moment, I may feel that I am adrift in the Jordan of death. Then I will feel a hand clasp mine, and I will know that it is the hand of my Saviour. Perhaps He will bear me across the river. Or He may lift me to my feet, and I will walk with Him on the surface of the river as Peter walked with Him on the waves of storm-tossed Galilee. In either case, we will step upon the shore of Immanuel's Land, and I will know I am home at last.

I will fall at the feet of Jesus and worship Him. Then He will lift me up and point to a city on a hill. People will be pouring out of the gates of the city and trooping down the hillside to meet me, and I will hear them shouting, "Welcome home! Welcome home, thou redeemed in the blood of the Lamb!"

And I will echo, "Home at last! Home at last!" That will be the first minute of the unending day of my new life of service for the Lord, who loved me and washed me from my sins.

Of course I look forward to seeing my loved ones in that land where we shall know as we also are known. There will be no parting over there and no sad good-byes. In that land where there is no night, we will never grow tired or weary. We will have time for each other. We will have time to worship and praise our Lord, and we will have time to do all the things we did not have time to do on earth. Eternity! Oh, eternity! *"And whosoever liveth and believeth in me shall never die . . ." (John 11:25).* Amen, and Amen.

Books by Dr. Louis Arnold

Thousands praise Dr. Arnold's books, and hundreds order them before they are off the press. People love both his novels and his Bible study books.

Great Inspirational Fiction

Readers appreciate the strong characters Dr. Arnold creates, his powers of description, and his gripping, emotion-filled stories.

Legend of Old Faithful, hardcover $19.99

Out of the Night, hardcover $19.99

Fathoms Deep, hardcover $19.99

Riverman, softcover .... $ 9.99

Riverman (Audio) read by author $12.99

SunshineValley, softcover .... $ 9.99

Euroclydon, softcover .... $ 9.99

Lucinda of Perryville, softcover .... $ 9.99

A Girl Named Candy, softcover .... $ 9.99

The Angel of Dragonpoint, softcover.... $ 9.99

Birdman, softcover .... $ 9.99

Other Arnold Books

Israeli Countdown to Eternity, softcover .. $ 9.99

When Will the Tribulation Begin? scover $ 9.99

Spiritual Realities, softcover .... $ 9.99

Day Starters, bestselling devotional, scover . $ 9.99

Family and Friends Cookbook (J. Arnold) . . . $ 9.99

Great Preachers I Have Known, scover . $ 9.99

Key to Understanding the Revelation, sc . $11.99

Arnold Publications --2440 Bethel Road --Nicholasville, KY 40356
Phone 1-800-854-8571